VIVIREMOS

VIVIREMOS
VENEZUELA VS. HYBRID WAR

EDITED BY
CLAUDIA DE LA CRUZ,
MANOLO DE LOS SANTOS,
VIJAY PRASHAD

INTERNATIONAL PUBLISHERS
New York

ISBN-10: 0-7178-0834-3 ISBN-13: 978-07178-0834-2

CONTENTS

PREFACE

Carlos Ron

I grew up hearing that the first country to stand up against neoliberalism was Venezuela. It took me some years to understand the meaning of the word "neoliberalism." But I do vividly remember when I learned what a sniper was. It was on 27 February 1989, the same year that I was later told History had ended, that History really began for me. I could see soldiers on the rooftop of the National Sports Institute looking on at protestors burning tires in front of a monument to the Carabobo battle which sealed Venezuela's independence in 1821. This event was part of the massive riots that later took the name of *Caracazo* and signified a poor people's rebellion against unbearable living costs, profound social exclusion and segregation, against children in the barrios having dog food as their best nutritional aspiration.

"Get out of the window before they think you are sniper!," shouted my grandmother across the living room. She was right to do so. What ensued the following weeks were a series of shootouts like I had never seen or heard before. The protests had no direction; there were no concrete demands and—even if they had them—there was no one to voice them. When repression struck, over 3,000 people died; no one was held responsible for the deaths. A decade of market reforms and more poverty followed, but Venezuela was fulfilling its role in the imperialist script. It has long been seen as the model democracy that would implement the appropriate policies that would take us to a new era of progress, and we could not allow the marginal populations to drag us back. In the long run, social differences would be overcome. In that long run, you know, when we are dead.

Nine years later, History was very much alive and in the making. The corrupt and inefficient political establishment that had created the conditions for the Caracazo, faced an unforgiving rejection at the polls. A former soldier, like the one I had seen on the rooftop, but who refused to use his weapons to repress hunger, was elected President with the overwhelming confidence of the Venezuelan people. The excluded now had a voice, a leader, a movement, and a political project: *Venezuela had a Revolution*. It was a revolution that ripped up Washington's script, blocked the privatization of the world's largest oil reserves, regained control of its industry, reduced poverty, overcame illiteracy, questioned media monopolies, enfranchised women, the indigenous, and the forgotten, got them Cuban doctors to see them for the first time in their lives, raised their levels of nutrition, and got them registered to vote and got them to believe in the Constitution as if it was a religious book. That "free-trade" model was abolished by ideas such as cooperation, solidarity, and complementarity. It had, above all, in Hugo Chávez a leader that was not afraid to seek help from Cuba, to sit down with Gaddafi or with Saddam Hussein to achieve higher oil prices. In other words, a revolution that proved that other worlds and ways are possible. Since the enthusiasm was contagious, soon labor unionists rose to power in Brazil and coca farmers in Bolivia, alternative economics reached office in Ecuador and liberation theology in Paraguay.

The empire felt something needed to be done and began a multi-form hybrid war against Venezuela. First, the obvious: a military coup in 2002 which failed to predict that both the military and the people would remain loyal to the Revolution. The empire moved to a next phase that, thanks to Wikileaks, was made public and which included: "penetrating Chávez's political base," "dividing Chavismo," "protecting vital U.S. business" and "isolating Chávez internationally." Election after election gave Chávez and the Bolivarian Revolution democratic victories in the hybrid war, but Chávez's death in 2013 meant that the "now or never" moment had come. The U.S. government, in its infinite lack of understanding of Venezuelan political reality, imagined that Venezuela's defiant path would end with Chávez. Once Nicolás Maduro was elected as his successor, an all-out war was put in motion.

Since his election, President Maduro has faced two insurrectional waves of political violence from extreme right groups in 2014 and 2017, an economic war with elements such as planned scarcity and induced inflation, the attempted use of lawfare tactics to overthrow him by the opposition-led National Assembly since 2015, an assassination attempt with drones in 2018, the self-proclamation of an illegal interim President promoted by Washington, an attempted coup in 2019, the announcement of indictments in the U.S. accusing him of drug trafficking, the incursion of mercenaries in 2020, just to name a few. Together with this, the Trump administration has employed its favorite tool in the box: the illegal, unilateral coercive measures they call "sanctions" in a misappropriation of a term given that only the U.N. Security

Council has the authority under international law to issue such measures.

For us, the people of Venezuela, the ones that dared to embark on a revolutionary path to reclaim social justice, the hybrid war has meant a direct attack on our greatest achievements: currently more than $5 billion of Venezuelan public funds are frozen in U.S. accounts. Companies that will trade oil for food, such as Mexico's Libre Abordo, were forced into bankruptcy by U.S. pressure. Banks do not even wish to transfer Venezuelan public funds because of the risks of being accused of collaborating with the "regime." Currency exchange fees needed to convert dollars into other currencies and avoid account freezes had a cost to the Venezuelan state equal to a year's supply of treatment for HIV patients that is provided for free. Delayed bank transactions for vaccine purchases prevented the timely start of vaccination campaigns. Key infrastructure has run down because companies that service them are forbidden to provide support, as in the case of power outages where General Electric can no longer offer its service. The stolen assets of Citgo Petroleum Corporation, a subsidiary of Venezuela's state oil company, no longer provide refined gasoline nor the cash needed to buy medicine for Venezuelans or to provide specialized medical treatment to patients that need bone marrow transplants. Tankers with imports aimed at resolving gasoline deficiencies are stopped and seized in the high seas by U.S. pirates claiming to be combatting drug trafficking. As a result, internal food distribution or mobilization for health care providers during the COVID-19 pandemic has been jeopardized. Life for everyday people has become a struggle, a challenge, and form of collective punishment for daring to rip up Washington's script.

This book speaks of the form in which imperialism manifests itself in our time. Trump has used unilateral coercive measures as his weapon of choice against anyone daring to act contrary to U.S. interests. These "sanctions" have been used to punish diplomacy, to punish the defense of human rights, to punish the convening of a National Constituent Assembly which proved effective in preventing the civil war that Washington wished to unleash, and more recently to punish even those in the opposition that dare to question the use of sanctions and the pain they cause as means of defeating Chavismo. This book, however, also speaks of the resilience of a people, their revolutionary project and their leadership in defending Venezuelan sovereignty for the last 21 years of constant and renewed aggression. Venezuela is an example of resilience and of political consciousness capable of writing new chapters in History. Chapters that will tell how the world's largest financial system cannot block solidarity and how no pressure is strong enough to break a people's dignity. This is our story, that of the Venezuelan people that in the middle of a menacing hybrid war, can still smile at you and say: *¡Viviremos . . . y venceremos!*

INTRODUCTION

Claudia De La Cruz, Manolo De Los Santos, and Vijay Prashad

For the past thirty years, the United Nations (U.N.) General Assembly has voted annually to strike down the unilateral, criminal U.S. blockade of Cuba. On November 7, 2019, 187 out of 193 states, led by the Group of 77, the Non-Aligned Movement, and all the other groups of the developing world, voted to end the blockade. Speaking of the embargo before the vote, Cuba's Foreign Minister Bruno Eduardo Rodríguez Parrilla said, "There is not a single Cuban family that has not endured its consequences." The blockade, he says, qualifies as an act of genocide under the 1948 Convention on the Prevention and Punishment of the Crime of Genocide.

Standing in the U.N. chamber, Venezuela's Minister for Foreign Affairs, Jorge Arreaza Montserrat said of the U.S. blockade on Cuba, "This is collective punishment because of the whims, capriciousness, and arrogance of those who believe they are superior." Foreign Minister Arreaza had in mind the United States of America, whose government was "trying to breathe life into the Monroe Doctrine." Articulated in 1823, the Monroe Doctrine announced that European influence was not to extend to the American hemisphere; the entire territory from Murchison Promontory (Canada) to Cape Froward (Chile) must demonstrate its suzerainty to the United States. It is this that Cuba (from 1959 onwards) and Venezuela (from 1999 onwards) have resisted. "We are free people," Foreign Minister Arreaza said, describing the U.S. policy towards Cuba as "economic and financial terrorism."

The Permanent Representative of the U.S. to the United Nations Kelly Craft defended the U.S. embargo of Cuba based on the principle of sovereignty. "We get to choose which countries we trade with," Ambassador Craft said. "This is our sovereign right."

Between two competing sovereignties, force decides.

Foreign Minister Arreaza spoke on behalf of Cuba, but he mentioned that the U.S. had recently tried to engineer a coup against the government of Venezuela. Both Cuba and Venezuela—who also have a "sovereign right" to "choose which countries [they] trade with"—face a suffocating set of policies driven by the United States government; neither Cuba nor Venezuela have been allowed to exercise their sovereignty through the use of force by the United States of America. This force comes in a variety of mechanisms, which includes economic and financial force, diplomatic force, ideological force, and military force. The combination of these various means to undermine the sovereignty of Cuba and Venezuela is known as the *hybrid war*. The United States of America has, as this book shows, prosecuted a hybrid war against Cuba for over sixty years and against Venezuela for over twenty years.

★

That the U.S. ambassador to the United Nations defends her government's blockade of Cuba based on its "sovereign right" to "chose which countries [they] trade with" suggests that there is no claim being made to ground the policy in international law; the argument made is that the U.S. reserves the sovereign right to do as it pleases. This is fair enough. But then this narrow defense is often larded with much nobler intentions, such as the promotion of human rights and democracy and the defense of international norms and international law. Neither the hybrid war on Cuba nor on Venezuela can be justified based on the vast—and not always clear—canons of international law, and certainly not on the sublime but unclear language of democracy and human rights.

Sanctions that are not imposed by the U.N. Security Council under Chapter VII of the U.N. Charter (1945) are not typically considered to be legal. In that Chapter of the Charter, there is a section that says, "The Security Council may decide what measures not involving the use of armed force are to be employed to give effect to its decisions." This suggests that the Security Council, where the United States has—from the collapse of the U.S.S.R. in 1991 to the recent past—exercised its authority, has the right to define when sanctions of various kinds are appropriate. But this is not the case from a close reading of the U.N. Charter, which puts limits on the power of the Security Council. For example, Article 55 in Chapter IX of the Charter calls upon the member states of the U.N. to promote "higher standards of living" and to find solutions to health problems; sanctions typically erode standards of living and disrupt health care systems, and therefore undermine these aspects of the Charter. It is also often forgotten that the U.N. Security Council is to operate based on the U.N.'s *Purposes and Principles* (Chapter I of the Charter) and that it is to report regularly to the General Assembly, which should be the higher body (this is in Article 24 in Chapter V).

Nonetheless, the U.S. sanctions on Venezuela currently do not have the imprimatur of a resolution by the United Nations. This is why Idriss Jazairy, the U.N. Special Rapporteur concerned with the negative impact of sanctions said, in January 2019, "I urge all countries to avoid applying sanctions unless approved by the United Nations Security Council, as required by the U.N. Charter." Jazairy, a veteran diplomat from Algeria, said, "I am especially concerned to hear reports that these sanctions are aimed at changing the government of Venezuela. Coercion, whether military or economic, must never be used to seek a change in government in a sovereign state. The use of sanctions by outside powers to overthrow an elected government is in violation of all norms of international law."

Outside the U.N. Charter, the Vienna Declaration and Programme of Action—which was adopted unanimously at the World Conference on Human Rights in Vienna on June 25, 1993—specifically cautioned states not to impose unilateral sanctions. It was based on this text that the U.N. created the Office of the High Commissioner for Human Rights. Article 31 of the Vienna Declaration is worth reproducing in full, since it lays out the legal basis for our claim in this book that the U.S. sanctions on Venezuela (and the U.S. embargo on Cuba) are a violation of international agreements and the spirit of the U.N. Charter:

> The World Conference on Human Rights calls upon States to refrain from any unilateral measure not in accordance

> with international law and the Charter of the United Nations that creates obstacles to trade relations among States and impedes the full realization of the human rights set forth in the Universal Declaration of Human Rights and international human rights instruments, in particular the rights of everyone to a standard of living adequate for their health and well-being, including food and medical care, housing and the necessary social services. The World Conference on Human Rights affirms that food should not be used as a tool for political pressure.

It is important to point out that the United States government is party to this Declaration. It says—without need for much clarification—that any "unilateral measure" that impinges on the "full realization of the human rights set forth in the Universal Declaration of Human Rights" is not to be utilized. The unilateral sanctions used against Venezuela as well as against thirty other countries certainly prevent the "full realization" of the human rights agenda; in fact, they have been shown by numerous studies to have reversed social gains made by these countries.

Michelle Bachelet, the former President of Chile and the High Commissioner of Human Rights, said, in August 2019, that the "sanctions are extremely broad and fail to contain sufficient measures to mitigate their impact on the most vulnerable sectors of the population." Bachelet's U.N. post was created by the Vienna Declaration, which warned about unilateral sanctions. "I fear that [the U.S. unilateral sanctions against Venezuela] will have far-reaching implications on the rights to health and to food in particular, in a country where there are already serious shortages of essential goods."

Based on the mandate of the Vienna Declaration, Bachelet further said, "There is a significant body of evidence showing that wide-ranging unilateral sanctions can end up denying people's fundamental human rights, including their economic rights as well as the rights to food and health, and could place obstacles to the delivery of humanitarian assistance." These comments, made before the announcement of the global pandemic in March 2020, have a special sharp resonance as the coronavirus continues its spread around the world.

On paper, the unilateral U.S. sanctions say that medical supplies are exempt from their various measures. But this is an illusion. For example, neither Venezuela nor Iran can easily buy medical supplies, nor can they easily transport them into their countries, nor can they use them in their largely public-sector health systems. In 2017, U.S. President Donald Trump enacted tight restrictions on Venezuela's ability to access financial markets; two years later, the U.S. government blacklisted Venezuela's central bank and put a general embargo against the Venezuelan state institutions. If any firm trades with Venezuela's public sector, it could face secondary sanctions. The U.S. Congress passed the Countering America's Adversaries Through Sanctions Act (CAATSA) in 2017, which tightened sanctions against Iran, Russia, and North Korea. The next year, Trump imposed a raft of new sanctions against Tehran that suffocated Iran's economy. Once more, access to the world banking system and threats to companies that traded with Iran made it almost impossible for Iran to do business with the world. In particular, the U.S. government made it clear that any business with the public sector of Iran and Venezuela was forbidden. The health infrastructure that provides for the mass of the populations in both Iran and Venezuela is run by the state, which means it faces disproportionate difficulty in accessing equipment and supplies, including testing kits and medicines. Countries sanctioned by the U.S. have struggled to import medical equipment and will struggle to access the vaccine for COVID-19. This pandemic reveals clearly the utterly immoral and unjust application of unilateral coercive sanctions by the United States against its political adversaries.

What provokes this hybrid war against Venezuela? Hugo Chávez won an immense landslide in 1998 in the presidential election. He came to office to undertake a project to democratize Venezuelan institutions and society, both through a new Constitution (1999) and through the mobilization of the population into new social forms (starting with Plan Bolivar in 1999). Resource socialism defined the government, which fought with the major North American and European multinational firms for a better deal for Venezuela. This entire orientation was called the Bolivarian Revolution. All this bothered the large capitalist firms, the local oligarchies, and the imperialist states. The U.S. backed a military coup against Chávez and the Bolivarian Revolution in 2002; the coup failed but it revealed that the U.S. government, and its allies, had no patience to see what kind of outcomes would emerge from the Bolivarian Revolution. The hybrid war against Venezuela and the Bolivarian Revolution was defined not to defend human rights or to defend Venezuelan democracy; it was entirely in the class interests of the Venezuelan oligarchy, the North American multinational firms, and the power of the imperialist bloc.

After that failed coup in 2002, the U.S. set-up a USAID/

Office of Transition Initiatives (OTI), funded various NGOs of the oligarchy, and worked to undermine the Bolivarian process. It was the U.S. that essentially shaped the Venezuelan "Opposition," with the USAID/OTI programme working to unify the fractured opposition groups and provide them with a coherent agenda. It was the USAID/OTI that claimed to have taught the Venezuelan opposition to undermine the democratic institutions by boycotting elections and arguing that the process was marked by fraud; this form of undermining the integrity of the process allowed the U.S. to promote the view—against all the available evidence—that the Venezuelan government was illegitimate. Knowing full well that the opposition could not win an election against the overwhelmingly popular Bolivarian process, the U.S. promoted the idea to destabilize democracy in Venezuela in the name of democracy. Calls to "protect" democracy and to create a "more open democratic system" came alongside the attempt to destroy the democratic institutions and the democratic spirit. The information war against Venezuelan democracy was a cornerstone of the hybrid war.

The leadership of Hugo Chávez in the region, including in the Caribbean, disturbed the regional oligarchy, the North American and European multinational corporations, and the imperialist states. That Chávez led the coalition against the U.S.-driven Free Trade Area of the Americas (2005) and that he drove an agenda to build alternative, Latin America-dominated regional institutions, greatly troubled Washington. It was even more disturbing in Washington to see Chávez craft socialist international trade regimes, such as through PetroCaribe with Haiti and Jamaica; these mechanisms provided trading relations outside market logics but driven by the consideration of development and solidarity. Such experiments had to be destroyed because they proved to be popular, and they proved that solidarity-defined trade was far better for the interests of poorer nations than market-driven trade and mild forms of aid.

The assault on Venezuela, as on Cuba, had nothing to do with grave violations of democracy and human rights. This was what Washington said, but this was not what worried the U.S. government; they worried precisely about the socialist character of the domestic and regional policy driven by Venezuela, and before that by Cuba. That is why these governments and their revolutionary developments had to be destroyed.

The depletion of the oil prices from 2009 threatened the Bolivarian process. Chávez died in 2013. The combination of low oil prices and the death of Chávez changed the political calculations.

Egged on by the United States, opposition leaders Leopoldo López and María Corina Machado called for demonstrations against the newly elected president Nicolás Maduro in 2014. It was clear that the protests were intended as a provocation, which allowed U.S. President Barack Obama to sign the Venezuela Defense of Human Rights and Civil Society Act of 2014. This act allowed Obama to sanction individuals in the Venezuelan government. The sanctions policy was to be the new lever to pressure Venezuela whose reliance on oil revenues—during low oil prices—left it already vulnerable. In March 2015, Obama declared Venezuela a "threat" to U.S. "national security," an extreme and unprovoked step, and sanctioned a handful of Venezuelan government officials.

The administration of Donald Trump sharpened and deepened the policy. Obama sanctioned seven individuals, while Trump sanctioned around a hundred individuals. Obama forged the spear; Trump has thrown it at the heart of Venezuela.

These early sanctions went after individuals, offering an inconvenience for some Venezuelan politicians and for sections of the state. The U.S. government would soon move the sanctions from individual inconvenience to social collapse. Trump's policy, from 2017, was to hit Venezuela's petroleum industry very hard. The U.S. government prevented Venezuelan government bonds from trading in U.S. financial markets, and then it prevented the state's energy company—PdVSA—from receiving payments for its export of petroleum products. The U.S. Treasury Department froze $7 billion in PdVSA assets, and it did not allow U.S. firms to export naphtha into Venezuela (a crucial input for the extraction of heavy crude oil).

The country relied on oil revenues to import food and medicines. The theft of the $7 billion in PdVSA assets, the seizure of 31 tonnes of Venezuelan gold (worth $1.95 billion in current prices) in the Bank of England, the transfer of ownership of the PdVSA subsidiary CITGO in the United States to the opposition and the pressure on oil exports squeezed Venezuela very hard. Former U.S. National Security Adviser John Bolton estimated that the United States (and Canadian) sanctions had cost Venezuela about $11 billion in just a few months.

When the United States began to put pressure on transportation firms to stop carrying Venezuelan oil, the schemes to export oil to the Caribbean (PetroCaribe) suffered, as did the fraternal delivery of oil to Cuba. This policy inflamed the situation in Haiti—which is in a long-term political crisis—and it has deepened the crisis in Cuba. The countries in the Caribbean, which relied upon Venezuelan oil, are now suffering deeply.

Economists Mark Weisbrot and Jeffrey Sachs calculated that the U.S. sanctions have resulted in the death of 40,000 Venezuelan civilians between 2017 and 2018. In their report—*Economic Sanctions as Collective Punishment: The Case of Venezuela* (April 2019)—they pointed out that this death toll is merely the start of what is to come. An additional 300,000 Venezuelans are at risk "because of lack of access to medicines or treatment," including 80,000 "with HIV who have not had antiretroviral treatment since 2017." There are 4 million people with diabetes and hypertension, most of whom cannot access insulin or cardiovascular medicine. "These numbers," they write, "by themselves virtually guarantee that the current sanctions, which are much more severe than those implemented before this year, are a death sentence for tens of thousands of Venezuelans."

Venezuela has imported food goods worth only $2.46 billion in 2018 compared to $11.2 billion in 2013. If food imports remain low and Venezuela is unable to hastily grow enough food, then—as Weisbrot and Sachs argue—the situation will contribute to "malnutrition and stunting in children."

In 2018, the U.N. High Commissioner for Human Rights Bachelet made the case that the cause of the deterioration of well-being in Venezuela predates the sanctions (a report from Human Rights Watch and Johns Hopkins University underlined this point). It is certainly true that the fall of oil prices had a marked impact on Venezuela's external revenues and the reliance upon food imports—a century-old problem—had marked the country before Trump's very harsh sanctions. But, the next year, Bachelet told the U.N. Security Council that "although this pervasive and devastating economic and social crisis began before the imposition of the first economic sanctions in 2017, I am concerned that the recent sanctions on financial transfers related to the sale of Venezuelan oil within the United States may contribute to aggravating the economic crisis, with possible repercussions on people's basic rights and well-being." A debate over whether it is mismanagement and corruption by the Maduro government or the sanctions that are the author of the crisis is largely irrelevant. The point is that a combination of the reliance on oil revenues and the sanctions policy has crushed the policy space for any stability in the country.

Weisbrot and Sachs say that these sanctions "would fit the definition of collective punishment," as laid out in the Hague Convention (1899) and in the Fourth Geneva Convention (1949). The United States is a signatory of both of these frameworks. "Collective penalties," says the Fourth Geneva Convention, "are prohibited." Tens of thousands of Venezuelans are dead. Tens of thousands more are under threat of death. Yet, no one has stood up against the grave breach of the convention in terms of collective punishment. There is not a whiff of interest in the U.N. Secretary General's office to open a tribunal on the accusations of collective punishment against Venezuela. Allegations of this seriousness are brushed under the rug.

Neither Cuba nor Venezuela has surrendered to U.S. pressure. Both with immense dignity have stood up to the blunt pressure exercised by the United States on behalf of its European, Canadian, and Latin American oligarchic allies. China, Iran, Russia, and other countries (including the ALBA bloc) have provided material support and acts of solidarity to allow both Cuba and Venezuela to survive this special period. On October 6, 2020, China's permanent representative to the United Nations—Zhang Jun—made a joint statement at the United Nations on behalf of 26 countries (including Iran and Venezuela) that are under U.S. sanctions. The "unilateral coercive measures" adopted by the United States, Ambassador Zhang said, "are contrary to the purpose and principles of the UN." It is fitting that Venezuela is leading a process on the international stage to create a coalition of states against the use of unilateral sanctions by the United States of America. Some of these countries met in 2019 with the intent of creating—through the Non-Aligned Movement—a platform of struggle against sanctions.

Such political formations are important, but they are insufficient. The U.S. is able to maintain a sanctions regime because of the dominance of the Dollar–Wall Street complex over the economic life of so many countries. The U.S. dollar denominates more than half of the world's trade, U.S. banking systems control the flow of money, the European SWIFT system provides the mechanism to transfer funds, firms that wish to trade with the U.S. worry about secondary sanctions, and so on. Unless alternative institutions are created—including non-dollar trade relations and a money wire service that is not dominated by the Atlantic powers—the vulnerability of countries to U.S. unilateral pressure will continue. This is why it has become imperative to create these new systems and institutions outside the control of Washington, such as new development banks, new international funding agencies, and new mechanisms for reconciliation of trade.

In these historic times of converging global crises, where humanity stands face-to-face with the implications of a failed global neoliberal system and the brutality of U.S. imperialism, it becomes urgent for communities to gain a deep understanding of the enemies of humanity and their tactics in order to become better equipped for our defense of life.

Viviremos: Venezuela vs. Hybrid War is a collective effort to contribute to our process of education and of organizing in the many communities in struggle. This edited collection comes from educators, intellectuals, workers, organizers, and movements around the world as an urgent call to focus attention on these cruel sanctions.

Our call is for the urgent need to strengthen our commitment to the study of the development of the hybrid war, to integrate our fight against imperialism—and sanctions—into all our work. Our call is for the principled unity and integration of our causes, the connection between struggles and communities to defend humanity against imperialist war.

Why focus on Venezuela? Venezuela is currently the epicenter of anti-imperialist resistance and is a representation of many communities in struggle. This book seeks to serve in deepening efforts of solidarity, and understanding the fight, resilience, and dignity of the Venezuelan people as an offering to our collective struggles and movements around the world.

Undoubtedly, we are living in a period of transitions, the

"interregnum" between the old world and the one struggling to be born. Consequently, as we work through many contradictions to resolve the needs of our communities, we are forced to rethink and adjust our actions to improve the existence of humanity.

History and our current conjuncture have taught us that we must seek a deeper understanding of our collective material reality in order to organize more strategically and efficiently. The need to understand ourselves as a global working class is crucial. We have been reminded that struggling together for our conceptual unity and taking collective action is the only key to ensure our survival.

Our positioning, but most importantly, our organized and collective actions, as communities in defense of human rights, democracy, and the sovereignty of nations, working towards the construction of peace and justice, is the determinant factor for our victory over systems of death and war.

Our hope is that beyond the reading of these essays, this book serves as an instrument of collective study, sparks constructive debate and conversations in many places, and informs our organizational and collective plans as we move to act in the advancement of our people's struggles.

Viviremos (We will live!) is not a simple proclamation, it is the determination of millions across the world who have been resisting U.S. imperialism. It is the commitment to defend the people's right to exist from those who seek to dismember the working class, our history and our advances.

We are grateful to the following for their solidarity and work that went into the production of this book: Manu Karuka, Aya Ouais, Ana Maldonado, David Shulman and Pluto Press, Sudhanva Deshpande and Nazeef Mollah of LeftWord Books, Gary Bono of International Publishers, Carlos Ron of the Instituto Simón Bolívar, and the staff of The People's Forum and the team at Tricontinental: Institute for Social Research.

THE MODUS OPERANDI OF CONTEMPORARY IMPERIALISM

Prabhat Patnaik

The process of accumulation under capitalism necessarily entails an exchange not just between the two departments of a closed capitalist economy, as Marx had sketched in Volume II of *Capital*, but also between the capitalist sector and its outlying regions. This exchange requires of course the opening of these outlying regions to capitalist penetration; in addition, however, it occurs not in a context of parallel or synchronous growth between these two segments, but, rather in a context where the capitalist sector keeps growing through accumulation, while the outlying regions remain more or less stagnant, so that the exchange between the two necessarily takes the form of the former forcibly squeezing out supplies from the latter. This phenomenon of a forcible squeezing out, rather than synchronous or parallel growth, is immanent in the nature of capitalism and constitutes the essence of imperialism. Imperialism is indeed a perennial accompaniment of capitalism.

Let us look at each of the assertions made above. The necessity for exchange between the capitalist sector and its outlying regions arises not just because the former needs the latter as its market, but also because it requires a host of raw materials which it can neither produce nor do without; in fact, the need for these raw materials continues to remain even after the markets provided by the outlying regions have gotten exhausted.

These raw materials, or primary commodities, are broadly of two kinds: those commodities which are the products of the tropical and semi-tropical land-mass and cannot be produced in the temperate regions which constitute the home base of capitalism (or can at best be produced only in certain seasons); and those commodities like oil and other minerals which constitute exhaustible resources.

In the case of tropical and semi-tropical products, the magnitude of land-mass on which such products are produced, generally within a system of peasant agriculture, is more or less used up, so that a rise in output entails an increasing (in fact steeply increasing) supply price. Such an increase in supply price would naturally begin to be anticipated by wealth-holders and hence destroy the monetary system of capitalism, as wealth-holders would change the form of their wealth-holding from money to such commodities.

Of course, the phenomenon of increasing supply price may be kept at bay if there is a steady increase in yields per hectare, or what may be called "land augmenting technological change," for then even the same land-mass can produce larger and larger amounts. Such technological change in the context of peasant agriculture, however, typically requires state initiative: for investing in irrigation; for promoting research and development; for developing better agricultural practices; for spreading such practices among the peasantry through a public extension service;

for providing assured remunerative prices to the peasants; for making cheap credit available; and so on; and such state initiative is something which capitalism is invariably against.

Not only is it against any direct state initiative and state spending per se, i.e. anything that is not mediated through the capitalists (for it undermines the social legitimacy of capitalism), but it is even more strongly against such initiative and spending that is directed toward raising the incomes of the peasant agriculture sector. The contrast between the phenomenon of growth in the capitalist sector and of stagnation in the peasant agriculture sector, which one typically encounters under capitalism, arises for this reason.

Given this contrast, tropical and semi-tropical products are obtained in adequate quantities for the requirements of a growing capitalist sector only by reducing their local absorption within these outlying regions themselves. This is achieved not through a profit inflation, which also threatens the value of money (except in war times when economic agents' asset choices are restricted), but through an income deflation imposed on the working people (workers, peasants, artisans, agricultural laborers) of the periphery, which squeezes their purchasing power and hence their absorption of such products. Imperialism is necessarily associated with the imposition of an income deflation on the working people of the periphery.

The second category of primary products, namely, exhaustible resources, also faces an increasing supply price, in the absence of a steady stream of innovations that keep economizing on their use, or of a steady development of substitutes that are no more expensive than the original resource, or of a steady discovery of new sources of minerals that are no more expensive. Now, while such discoveries of new sources, or development of substitutes do occur, there is no certainty about them. To keep the phenomenon of increasing supply price at bay, and also to ensure that their price is kept suitably low for the capitalist sector, income deflation on the outlying producing region is invariably imposed by the former on the latter. This is done for restricting local absorption; and one way it is done, among others, is through keeping down the locally retained price.

An income deflation imposed by the metropolis on the periphery therefore is a ubiquitous phenomenon under capitalism and constitutes the essence of imperialism. But while this is true in general, the precise manner in which this income deflation is imposed, and supplies are squeezed out from the periphery keeps changing throughout the history of capitalism and needs to be specifically examined for each phase.

I

Colonialism imposed this income deflation quite openly: the instrument of coercion was through the open exercise of political power; and the modus operandi of income deflation was through the open use of three distinct processes: capturing the natural resources of the periphery by metropolitan companies; "the drain of wealth," which meant a transfer of the tropical colony's or semi-colony's surplus to the metropolis without any quid pro quo; and "deindustrialization," which meant the displacement of local artisan production by imported manufactured goods from the metropolis.

In the post-colonial period, there was an effort on the part of the Third World to break out of the syndrome of income deflation, and the pattern of international division of labor that had been imposed upon it during the colonial era. This was done through the adoption of measures such as protecting the domestic producers against the import of metropolitan products (and also of special measures to protect domestic petty producers from domestic large-scale manufacturing); the snatching back of control over the country's mineral resources from the metropolitan corporations; and the introduction of land-augmenting technological change that raised per hectare yields in agriculture, including in particular peasant agriculture.

As a result, while metropolitan demands for tropical products continued to be met without any significant rise in their prices, so that capitalism was not unduly inconvenienced on this score, this occurred within a framework of *dirigiste* development in the Third World; and since the same *dirigiste* strategy also entailed metropolitan capitalism's losing control over the erstwhile colony's natural resources, it put up a fierce resistance against this strategy. The imperialist camp, led by the United States, was continuously engaged in a bitter struggle against Third World anti-imperialist nationalism which was expressed through such a *dirigiste* strategy. This struggle frequently led to U.S. efforts (or efforts by other metropolitan powers with U.S. blessings) to topple *dirigiste* regimes in the Third World.

Two aspects of such efforts, however, should be noted. One, they were more political than economic, since economic instruments like sanctions were quite ineffective at that time. This was partly because the Soviet Union existed and provided a source of support in the face of imperialist sanctions, and partly also because the sanctions just tried to do what the Third World regimes were attempting to do anyway.

Preventing such regimes from buying Western goods could hardly constitute a threat when the Third World economies themselves were trying to develop the domestic production of precisely those goods whose supplies were to be restricted through sanctions. True, preventing the purchase of Third World goods by metropolitan powers would constitute a source of difficulty for Third World economies, but this is exactly where the Soviet Union was useful for providing an alternative market. The case of Cuba is a classic example of this.

Inconvenient regimes, therefore, could not be brought to their knees merely through the use of the economic instrument; they had to be toppled and the typical method chosen for this was the *coup d'état*. The *coup d'état*, however, meant that the toppling could not be done in the name of "defending democracy." The regime being toppled was itself democratically elected, such as that of Mossadegh or Arbenz or Allende, while what was substituted in its place by the imperialist-promoted *coup d'état* was invariably an authoritarian one.

The immediate post-colonial period therefore saw a loosening of imperialist control over the Third World. The coups of the period that imperialism resorted to against popularly elected governments were a reflection of this fact. This, while it prevented imperialism from claiming any high moral ground, such as "defending democracy," also made imperialism in popular perception synonymous with perennial attempts to effect *coups d'état*, so much so that in the next phase of capitalism when neoliberal policies held sway and there was hardly much need for such *coups d'état* any longer, many came to believe that imperialism itself had disappeared.

Frequent *coups d'état* in other words belong to an era when imperialist control was being loosened, *against the wishes of imperialism*; but by identifying the very phenomenon of imperialism with *coups d'état*, an occurrence true of the period of weakening imperialism was mistaken as the essence of imperialism, while the period of powerful imperialist hegemony, which is what characterizes the neoliberal era, was seen to be symptomatic of the very end of imperialism itself. This is the problem that arises when one defines a phenomenon solely by certain symptoms and not by its essential underlying relationships.

II

In fact, in the period of neoliberalism, since the avowed objective of the economic regime is to enhance mutual interdependence through trade, as opposed to promoting self-reliance which was the concern of the post-colonial *dirigisme*, the economic weapon of sanctions becomes particularly powerful; and the absence of the Soviet Union further enhances its potency. The opening of the economy to free flows of goods and services increases the economy's dependence on imports, and correspondingly on exports as well; and this is precisely why any curbs on imports or on exports hurts a nation far more than it would have hurt in an earlier period when it was attempting to be self-reliant.

Likewise, freer flows of capital, especially of finance, also make the economy far more vulnerable to imperialist arm-twisting which obviates to a great extent any need for direct imperialist political or military intervention. Under the neoliberal regime the snatching back of control over its natural resources from foreign capital by a Third World economy is anyway reversed to a large extent, so that the same objective for which *coups d'état* were engineered earlier is now achieved peacefully with the consent of the country concerned. Additionally, if perchance a government that comes to power wishes to undo what neoliberalism had effected, then the outflow of finance in sheer response to it is usually enough to bring that government to its knees and force it to abandon its plans.

In short, imperialism in the neoliberal era has little reason to resort to political or military intervention in the Third World; the spontaneous working of the economic processes is sufficient to ensure that no country, once it has been drawn into the vortex of imperialist "globalization," has the temerity to go back upon it; the costs of transition to be paid for any retreat from "globalization" are simply forbiddingly great.

Nonetheless, occasionally some Third World country shows the resilience to persist with an agenda of delinking from imperialist "globalization" despite all the transitional difficulties it faces. In such cases imperialism feels the need for political intervention, and in case this too fails, then military intervention. But precisely because the transitional difficulties of delinking bring distress to the people, and hence some degree of dissatisfaction among them and a certain loss of popular support for the government in question, it becomes possible for imperialism to pass off its intervention as being in the "interests of the people" themselves.

Since under the democratic government which sought to effect a delinking from imperialist globalization, people enjoy the right to hold demonstrations and express their anger against the hardships they face (because of these transitional difficulties), this expression is interpreted in exaggerated terms by imperialism as showing a lack of trust in the government by the *people as a whole.* Any contrary indication that the government actually enjoys the trust of the majority, which may be given by counter-demonstrations by the people in support of the government, or by election results favorable to the ruling government, are dismissed as being inauthentic, as being simply "orchestrated" or manipulated by the government. The entire metropolitan media, including even the liberal newspapers, start a chorus that "democracy is being violated."

Hence, imperialist political intervention against a government attempting to delink from imperialist "globalization" is passed off as a "defense of democracy." Even military intervention is passed off as being in defense of democracy, in sharp contrast to the interventions during the period of post-colonial *dirigisme* which neither made, nor could possibly make, any such claim. The wheel, in short, comes full circle in the neoliberal era where democracy comes to be defined as being synonymous with the rule of capital and hence the hegemony of imperialism; any attempt to break out of this comes to be presented as *anti-democratic.*

Imperialist intervention in Latin America of late demonstrates this change in the situation, compared to the era of post-colonial *dirigisme*, a change that buttresses the position of international finance capital in maintaining its hegemony. Some intrepid Third World governments, however, have continued to defy imperialism despite these odds. And the foremost example of such defiance is what is shown by President Nicolás Maduro of Venezuela and the people of Venezuela under his leadership. In what follows I shall give a brief account of the Venezuelan people's struggle against imperialism and the changed tactics used by the latter which we have just been discussing.

III

What is happening in Venezuela today provides an object lesson on the nature of imperialist intervention in Third World countries in the era of neoliberalism. Imperialism has of late intervened along similar lines in other Latin American countries, notably Brazil; but Venezuela, precisely because of the strong resistance it has put up, shows the techniques of imperialism in sharper relief.

Not long ago, the leftward turn in Latin America, not just Cuba, Bolivia, and Venezuela, but Brazil, Argentina, Ecuador, and several other countries where left-of-center regimes had come to power and pursed redistributive policies in favor of the working poor, had been a source of inspiration for progressive forces all over the world. Today, many of these regimes have been toppled, not because their programs and policies have lost popular support, but through vile machinations in which the United States has played a major role. They have been *coups d'état* of a new kind, different from the earlier ones effected by the United States in the 1950s, 1960s, and 1970s; they are specific to the era of neoliberalism.

There have been two important factors contributing toward this toppling. One is the collapse of the primary commodity terms of trade in the wake of the world capitalist crisis. Latin American countries, including even Brazil, have been heavy raw material exporters, and the adverse terms of trade movement has left them with reduced foreign exchange earnings for buying their essential imports. In the case of Venezuela, reduced oil prices have played this role; reduced oil prices have also reduced government revenues. The government's attempt to preserve the redistributive benefits enjoyed by the poor in the face of such a decline in foreign exchange earnings, instead of its adopting "austerity" measures, which is what imperialist agencies advocate, has caused a spurt of inflation.

This has undoubtedly meant hardships for the poor. But these hardships, one must note, have not been because of the *policies*; they have been caused by the decline in terms of trade. In fact, the poor would have suffered far more in the event of a policy of "austerity" in the face of these difficulties than they have through the non-imposition of such a policy of "austerity."

The economic difficulties for Venezuela have been infinitely worsened because of the sanctions imposed by the United States which prevent even essential commodities like life-saving drugs from being imported freely. And of late the United States has further escalated its economic war against Venezuela by freezing the assets held by the Venezuelan state-owned oil company in the United States, and announcing that all revenues from Venezuelan oil exports to the United States will be given not to the democratically elected and constitutionally legitimate regime of President Nicolás Maduro, but to the regime of Juan Guaidó, who, with U.S. backing, has simply proclaimed himself as the president. This amounts literally to stealing Venezuela's own money to stage a coup in Venezuela itself, a phenomenon reminiscent of the colonial era when the colonial people were plundered to finance colonial conquests.

Such stealing, and sanctions, needless to say, compound the misery of the people of Venezuela, and this very misery is then blamed on the Maduro government to turn people against it.

The second element that has contributed to the recent toppling game is the fact that the United States is now gradually disengaging itself from direct involvement in the Middle East, *without in anyway giving up its imperial pursuits there.* And this now allows it to focus more on Latin America.

The recent U.S. coup attempts, of which Venezuela is a classic example, differ from the U.S.-sponsored coups of the 1950s, 1960s, and 1970s in at least six obvious ways and constitute an altogether new pattern. We have already noted these differences earlier and will illustrate our earlier assertions with evidence from Latin America.

The first is that while the earlier coups, whether in Iran or Guatemala, or Chile, had been against democratically elected governments, and had unashamedly installed in their place U.S.-backed authoritarian regimes, the current coups, though also directed against democratically elected governments, are carried out in the name of democracy. In Brazil, Bolsonaro appears as a democratically elected president; not only, however, was there a "parliamentary coup" against Dilma Rousseff, but the political leader acknowledged to be the most popular one in the country, namely, ex-president Luiz Inácio Lula da Silva of the Workers' Party, was not even allowed to contest the presidential elections.

Likewise, in Venezuela, Juan Guaidó, the U.S.-backed pretender happens to be the president of the National Assembly, and not just some military strongman. In other words, the political forces representing the old exploitative white-supremacist order are being directly mobilized en masse by the United States in this struggle against the progressive regimes in Latin America.

Associated with this is the phenomenon of large-scale street protests and demonstrations organized by the U.S.-backed forces which claim to be defending democracy even though they are arrayed against the legal democratically elected governments. Counter-revolutionary coups, in short, have acquired a mass character instead of being mere military putsches, as was the case earlier.

Second, these counter-revolutionary mass uprisings derive sustenance from the economic difficulties faced by the people, even though progressive governments are not responsible for these difficulties, and even though most of these difficulties are created through the deliberate activities of U.S. imperialism itself. The coups of the earlier era neither had a mass character, nor followed the outbreak of any economic difficulties, nor even bothered to justify themselves by invoking these difficulties. True, Dr. Cheddi Jagan's government in Guyana was toppled through the unleashing of a truckers' strike which was financed by imperialism. But what was occasionally used then is the norm now.

Third, the economic difficulties, though largely created by imperialism itself, in addition to the functioning of the world capitalist economy, are blamed not only on the progressive governments, but more explicitly on their left-wing policies. Economic difficulties are attributed to the nationalization of mineral resources, to state intervention in the economy, to the anti-capitalist policy stances, and so on. The propaganda for the coup incorporates an ideological attack on any interference with the functioning of the neoliberal order. This ideological attack is necessarily fuzzy. It invokes concepts like "corruption," and "incompetence," but these are supposed to be synonymous with state interference with the neoliberal order.

Fourth, by the same token, the coup explicitly puts forward an agenda which involves the restoration of the pro-corporate neoliberal order. A plan for "Democratic Transition" put forward in Venezuela, for instance, which outlines what the coup will do, includes: (i) The reactivation of the productive apparatus (by accessing IMF funds); (ii) the removal of all controls, regulations and "bureaucratic obstacles, and punitive measures"; (iii) international investment within a regulatory framework that creates confidence and effective protection of private property; (iv) opening for private investment in public enterprises; (v) approval of a new Hydrocarbon Law that would allow private capital to hold majority shares in oil projects; (vi) the private sector will be responsible for the operation of utility assets; (vii) efficiency in order to reduce the size of the state.

This is an unashamedly neoliberal agenda; yet it constitutes the program of the coup. Such a clear message that the democratically elected government should be overthrown in order to push a corporate agenda has never been given so explicitly before.

Fifth, current coups proceed on the basis of the backing of all the imperialist powers, even though they may be effected by the United States. Thus, the European Union was asked by President Trump to recognize the pretender Juan Guaidó's government as the legitimate government of Venezuela, and it duly did. It is a sign of the times, both of the fact that the United States itself does not have the same strength as it had before, and also of the fact that we live in a world where inter-imperialist rivalries are muted, that the cooperation of the others is required by the United States even when it undertakes an imperialist action.

And finally, the case of Venezuela shows the important role that the media are now playing in softening people into accepting that an imperialist action against an elected Third World government constitutes a defense of democracy. Newspapers from the *New York Times* down have been pushing this line.

We have in short, a new world order now where the equating of corporate interests with democracy is becoming an accepted principle. The Venezuelan people have stood firm until now against the U.S.-sponsored coup; because of this, the United States is now threatening them with armed intervention. If armed intervention comes about, then it will be the first such action in recent years against a sovereign country, not on the grounds, no matter how flimsy, that it poses a security threat to the United States or that it has somehow harmed U.S. interests, but simply on the grounds that it has dared to depart from a regime of neoliberalism.

SANCTIONS UNDER THE SHADOW OF ANTI-COLONIALISM

Vijay Prashad

LAWS FOR EUROPEAN WARS

In the old days, in the days of colonialism, there was no need for any justification. If a colonial power wanted to invade a territory, it could do so at will. Other colonial powers could object—and sometimes did—but this objection did not come on behalf of those who were being overrun; it came out of the competitive feeling between colonial powers. There was no need for any legal framework for these interventions, nor was there any barrier to wholesale massacres.

The first Geneva Convention (1864) emerged out of a sense of disquiet at the large numbers of Europeans killed in battles in Europe. Two particular engagements disgusted the public: the conflict in Crimea between 1853 and 1856, which claimed over 300,000 lives, and the Battle of Solfernino in 1859, which claimed 40,000 lives in a single day. Out of these two wars came the First Geneva Convention and the International Committee for Relief to the Wounded (later the International Committee of the Red Cross). This law and this institution set the moral framework for warfare.[1]

It would all fall apart during the First World War, when the technology of war exceeded any moral framework. Chemical weapons and aerial bombardment removed the "honor" in warfare, making combat a matter of technological superiority rather than bravery. The impact of aerial bombardment was the most significant, since it meant that the divide between combatant and civilian began to dissolve in front of the technological ability to bomb civilian areas far behind the frontlines of the battlefield. Several new Geneva Conventions (1929, 1949) would follow, each trying to ameliorate the harshness of the new technologies of death. The Nazis had no qualms about civilian deaths, the prelude being the bombing of Guernica (Spain) in 1937. But the Allies were no less harsh. In 1942, the British government acknowledged that its bombing was to damage "the morale of the enemy civil population and, in particular, the industrial workers."[2]

The new technology of warfare—and the Holocaust—demanded that the West create the United Nations, and the U.N. Charter (1945).

LAWLESS COLONIAL WARS

Discussions around the First Geneva Convention in 1864 made no mention of the colonial wars. There was nothing about the terrible repression against the Indian uprising of 1857, nothing about the savagery in the crackdown against

1 Dietrich Schindler and Jiří Toman, eds., *The Laws of Armed Conflicts: A Collection of Conventions, Resolutions, and Other Documents* (Leiden: Martinus Nijhoff Publishers, 1988), 280–1.

2 United Kingdom Air Ministry, *Area Bombing Directive*, General Directive no. 5, S.46368/D.C.A.S., February 14, 1942.

uprisings of enslaved people in the Americas, nothing about the genocidal killings of Indigenous peoples in Australia and the Americas—silence.

The silence would run from 1864 through 1929 and then into the 1949 Geneva Conventions. There is nothing to cite here to show that there is this silence—only that there are *no* references to any colonial wars in these laws of war. It was only in 1977—as Additional Protocol I—that the Geneva process acknowledged that wars of national liberation were to be considered as armed conflicts under the framework of the Conventions. But that was only because the formerly colonized, newly independent states in the Non-Aligned Movement—formed in 1961—*fought* to bring in this addition.[3]

In the colonies, all interventions were legal, all attacks and massacres were legal. If the natives misbehaved, the colonizer could do what they wanted. The term "gunboat diplomacy" exemplifies the nature of the lawlessness. Sometimes the liberal conscience had to confront its own brutality. Then, justifications had to be conjured up. In 1923, British officials in London worried about the harshness of their operations in Afghanistan. But after a brief discussion, they concurred that international law—the Geneva Conventions—was not applicable "against savage tribes who do not conform to codes of civilized warfare."[4]

That brutality would run long past the creation of the

[3] *Offcial Records of the Diplomatic Conference on the Reaffirmation and Development of International Humanitarian Law applicable in Armed Confücts*, vol. I (Bern: Federal Department of Foreign A5airs, 1978), 115–84.

[4] AIR 5/1328, Air Sta5, Employment of Aircraft on the North-West Frontier of India, March 1, 1924, 8e National Archives, Kew, United Kingdom, 2.

United Nations, long past the slogan of "never again" that came out of disgust at the Holocaust. During Britain's genocidal war in Kenya from 1952 to 1960, the colonial police chief Ian Henderson led the most brutal "pseudo-gangster operation." Henderson's book—published to great acclaim in 1958—was called *Man Hunt in Kenya*; he was after terrorists and savages, and his attitude was fully in the saddle as he prosecuted one of the ugliest colonial wars of the twentieth century.[5]

NATIVES AND THE UNIVERSAL

Gradually, and with intensity, movements for national liberation grew across the colonized world. These movements did not merely demand political freedom against the colonial regimes. We are part of the human race, they said, and therefore we are part of universal ideas of freedom and humanity. This was the essence of the resolutions that emerged from the League Against Imperialism meeting held in Brussels in 1927–28. The political resolution amplified this demand with its anger at the "reign of terror" and "brutal measures of repression" used against the national liberation movements from Nicaragua to India. Nothing, it was felt, can stand in the way of the demands of humanity to walk freely onto the stage of history.[6]

Over the decades that followed, national liberation

5 Ian Henderson, *Man Hunt in Kenya* (New York: Doubleday and Company, 1958).

6 Resolution, "Political Resolution of the General Council of the League against Imperialism," 1927, General Council of the League against Imperialism Brussels Conference, League Against Imperialism Archives, International Institute of Social History, Amsterdam, Netherlands.

movements grew in strength, endured vicious attacks by the imperialists, and developed their own understanding of the essential unity of humanity. The racism of colonialism was not to be mirrored in the national liberation movements, which fought for universality and not for their own particular advancement.

The 1941 Atlantic Charter, pushed by U.S. President F.D. Roosevelt, came with all the high-minded principles of universality that mirrored the demands of the national liberation movements. But, like U.S. President Woodrow Wilson's 14 Points (1918), Roosevelt's Charter was more bombast than reality. Anxiousness about anti-colonialism impacted the highest reaches of the imperialists—Wilson worried about the revolutions in Mexico (2010), China and India (1911), as well as the Russian Revolution (1917); Roosevelt saw history in the face and it revealed that anti-colonialism would prevail after the Second World War ended. British Deputy Prime Minister Clement Attlee went before a group of West African students—electric with their hope for freedom from colonialism—in 1941 to say, "The Atlantic Charter: it means dark races as well. Coloured people as well as white will share the benefits of the Churchill-Roosevelt Atlantic Charter."[7] His Prime Minister Winston Churchill did not share this view. In 1942, he announced as the Allies landed in North Africa, "I have not become the King's First Minister in order to preside over the liquidation of the British Empire."[8] Imperialists had to acknowledge the rising power of national liberation, but they were not going to give

[7] "The Atlantic Charter: It Means Dark Races Too," *Daily Herald*, August 16, 1941, 1.

[8] Winston Churchill, "The End of the Beginning," Speech, London, November 10, 1942.

in without a brutal fight.

Just as Ho Chi Minh announced freedom for Indochina in 1945, French troops returned to retake the region, as they did in Algeria. The British would fight brutally to hold on to Malaya and Kenya but would accept the partition of India as long as their airbases in northern Pakistan remained in the country. Flag freedom was permitted, but the newly freed countries were under economic and political pressure to hastily join up to the imperialist military alliances (CENTO, SEATO). The principle contradiction in the years after 1945 was not along the axis of West-East—the Cold War—but between North-South—the war against decolonization.

Roosevelt saw that the structural basis of the North-South divide, or more properly the West-South divide, was war. When he visited Gambia, then a British colony, in 1943 after the Casablanca Conference with Churchill, Roosevelt noted, "The thing is, the colonial system means war. Exploit the resources of an India, a Burma, a Java; take all the wealth out of these countries, but never put anything back into them, things like education, decent standards of living, minimum health requirements—all you're doing is storing up the kind of trouble that leads to war."[9] This was not all high moral principle, but an acknowledgment of reality. Roosevelt had seen this pressure from Latin America, which had moved him to the Good Neighbor Policy of 1933 that pledged non-intervention in the hemisphere in exchange for drawing resources toward the war effort. Pressure from the national liberation movements and the resistance to intervention (in Nicaragua and Haiti) forced the imperialists to come to terms with the changing balance of forces. Even Gambia, which is

[9] Quote by Franklin D. Roosevelt in Elliott Roosevelt, *As He Saw It* (New York: Duell, Sloan and Pearce, 1946), 74.

not often considered a major frontline of the anti-colonial movement, was home to the Bathurst Trade Union, which—with some assistance from the League Against Imperialism—led a general strike in 1929–30. This strike startled London, where the officials hastily tried to control the situation by recognizing the rights of trade unions and trying to buy off union leaders (through the Passfield Memorandum of 1930). But, as the communist leader George Padmore wrote in *The Life and Struggle of Negro Toilers*, these strikes—including in Gambia—were "taking on more and more of an anti-imperialist character."[10]

The native said it was part of the universal. That had to be recognized.

THIRD WORLD PROJECT

In December 1960, the United Nations General Assembly passed a resolution on decolonization. "The process of liberation," agreed the nations of the world, "is irresistible and irreversible."[11] This resolution was the summary of major fights from Cuba to Vietnam, from Indonesia to Egypt. Over the course of the 1960s, a broad understanding emerged in the former colonial world about the necessity of freedom from colonialism and from imperialism. The temperament of the various national liberation struggles differed based on the class alignment of their leading organizations. It is this difference that fractured the new nations in the anti-

10 George Padmore, *The Life and Struggle of Negro Toilers* (London: Red International of Labour of Unions Magazine for the International Trade Union Committee of Negro Workers, 1931).

11 G.A. Res. 1514 (XV), 9, U.N. Doc. A/RES/1514 (December 14, 1960), https://undocs.org/en/A/RES/1514(XV), accessed March 15, 2020.

colonial world. There were rightward leaning states and leftward leaning states, but each of them—from Saudi Arabia to Tanzania—would remain within the Non-Aligned Movement (NAM), created in 1961. By 1973, even the rightward states would acknowledge the radical agenda set by the NAM in its New International Economic Order (NIEO). Indeed, even countries like Saudi Arabia and Brazil—steeped in monarchies and military dictatorships—found merit in the argument that the global economic and political order needed to be reformed.

New states that won their independence after the Second World War gathered at Bandung (Indonesia) in 1955. There they laid out the outlines of what would be considered a "non-aligned" foreign policy. It was these states—notably Egypt, India, and Yugoslavia—that led the way for the creation of the Non-Aligned Movement in 1961 and that same year the Committee of 24 or the Decolonization Committee in the United Nations. This inter-state movement had a cognate in the United Nations through the Group of 77 (G-77), formed in 1964 at the U.N. Conference of Trade and Development. It was out of their agenda that the guts of the NIEO was crafted: subsidies and tariffs to grow national economies, cartels to protect prices of exported raw minerals, preferential financing to go around the prohibitive rates set by banks, and so on.[12]

By the mid-1960s, the NAM was challenged on its right and left flanks. From the right came NAM states that had formed close associations with imperialism, whether

[12] G.A. Res. 3201 (S-VI), U.N. Doc. A/RES/S-6/3201 (May 1, 1974); G.A. Res. 3202 (S-VI), U.N. Doc. A/RES/S-6/3202 (May 1, 1974); G.A. Res. 3281 (XXIX), U.N. Doc. A/RES/29/3281 (December 12, 1974).

by joining the Manila or Baghdad "security" pacts or by the formation in 1969 of the Organization of Islamic Cooperation (led by Saudi Arabia, Morocco, and Pakistan). These formations took a position against Third World-style socialism and communism. From the left came the Tricontinental, a group established by Cuba, of state and national liberation movements that believed in a fuller freedom—often to be attained by armed struggle. The Tricontinental would not only gather heads of states, but leaders of national liberation movements from Cape Verde to Vietnam. At the 1966 Tricontinental Conference in Havana, Cuba's President Osvaldo Dorticós Torrado, who had been present at the NAM's founding in Belgrade, was crisp in his denunciation of the mood and strategy of conciliation to imperialism—"The problem of underdevelopment, even of independent nations, cannot be solved with palliatives, with institutions and technical instruments that emerge out of international conferences. The cause of underdevelopment is none other than the subsistence of imperialist domination, and thus it can be overcome only through a struggle against and by total victory against imperialism."[13] These were strong words. By the 1970 NAM meeting in Zambia and the 1973 NAM meeting in Algiers, the ethos of the Tricontinental would be center stage.[14]

13 Osvaldo Dorticós Torrado, *First Solidarity Conference of the Peoples of Africa, Asia and Latin America* (Havana: OSPAAAL, 1966).

14 "Lusaka Declarations, 1970" Adopted by the Third Conference of the Heads of State or Government of Non-Aligned Countries, Lusaka, September 10, 1970, NAM Summits: Official Documents, James Martin Center for Nonproliferation Studies, http://cns.miis.edu/nam/documents/Official_Document/3rd_Summit_FD_Lusaka_Declaration_1970.pdf, accessed March 15, 2020; "Documents of the Fourth Conference of Heads of State or Government of Non-Aligned

Cuba's revolution of 1959 could not be contained. While Castro and Dorticós laid out their vision of armed struggle on a global scale, Che Guevara was absent from Havana. He was on a secret mission in Tanzania to assist the resistance movement in the Congo. Che was disappointed. "The human element failed," he wrote in his *Congo Diary*. "There is no will to fight. The leaders are corrupt. In a word, there was nothing to do."[15] He would draft two books on economics and philosophy before moving on to his tragic mission in Bolivia. All this was supported by the Cuban government. The export of revolution, the Cuban leadership felt, was the essence of their revolution. At the Tricontinental conference in 1966, Castro announced that this new body would "coordinate support for revolutionary wars of liberation throughout the colonized world." Cuba would provide logistical support and people to all liberation movements "within her means, wherever they occur."[16]

The imperative of armed struggle at the Tricontinental came fully developed from the PAIGC's Amilcar Cabral,[17] who argued that "we are not going to eliminate imperialism by shouting insults against it. For us, the best or worst shout against imperialism, whatever its form, is to take up arms

Countries," Algiers, September 5–9, 1973, NAM Summits: Official Documents, James Martin Center for Nonproliferation Studies, http://cns.miis.edu/nam/documents/Official_Document/4th_Summit_FD_Algiers_Declaration_1973_Whole.pdf, accessed March 15, 2020.

15 Ernesto Che Guevara, *Congo Diary: Episodes of the Revolutionary War in the Congo* (Melbourne, Victoria: Ocean Press, 2012).

16 Fidel Castro, First Solidarity Conference of the Peoples of Africa, Asia and Latin America.

17 African Party for the Independence of Guinea and Cape Verde.

and fight."[18] Cabral picked up the gun not out of choice, but out of necessity. The PAIGC began its independence struggle in Guinea-Bissau and Cape Verde in 1956. Three years later, the Portuguese authorities conducted a massacre at Pijiguiti, killing 50 unarmed dockworkers. It was this colonial violence that pushed the PAIGC into the armed struggle that ran from 1961 to 1974. It was imperialism's harsh face that moved the national liberation struggles of the 1960s and the 1970s into the armed phase. It was the viciousness of imperialism that denied the national aspirations of the people of places like Vietnam and the Congo to move to the gun. An inventory of that colonial violence would include the Malayan Emergency (1948–60), the Kenyan Emergency (1952–60), the French war on Algeria (1954–62), the French war on Vietnam (1946–54), the U.S. war on Vietnam (1954–75), the failed 1961 U.S. invasion of Cuba at the Bay of Pigs, the 1961 assassination of the Congo's Patrice Lumumba, the U.S. invasion of Guatemala (1954) and the Dominican Republic (1965), and the massacre of the Communists in Indonesia (1965). In the lead-up to the Tricontinental, in October 1965 French intelligence and Moroccan intelligence assassinated Mehdi Ben Barka, one of the planners of the Tricontinental. What different kind of futures might have been available to the Congo and to Morocco had the Congolese National Movement and the National Union of Popular Forces in Morocco been able to triumph? Such different futures buried with the corpses of those who had been assassinated. It was

[18] Amilcar Cabral, "The Weapon of Theory," Address delivered to the First Tricontinental Conference of the Peoples of Asia, Africa and Latin America held in Havana in January 1966, www.marxists.org/subject/africa/cabral/1966/weapon-theory.htm, accessed June 29, 2020.

this colonial violence that set the tactical terms for the armies of national liberation that came to Havana in 1966.

The violence of the armies of national liberation was, as Amilcar Cabral put it, "to answer the criminal violence of the agents of imperialism. Nobody can doubt that, whatever its local characteristics, imperialist domination implies a state of permanent violence against the nationalist forces."[19] Violence is the essence of imperialism and it is the instinct of a cornered imperialist bloc. It was this violence that was on display in the Vietnamese village of My Lai in March 1968. One soldier described his mission with brutal honesty: "Our mission was not to win terrain or seize positions, but simply to kill: to kill Communists and to kill as many of them as possible. Stack 'em like cordwood."[20] Four years later, in 1972, Portuguese colonial troops went into the village of Wiriyamu in Mozambique and massacred between 150 and 300 villagers. Before they killed them, the Portuguese colonial troops made the villagers clap their hands and say goodbye.[21]

By 1975, the Vietnamese had defeated the Americans, and Portugal was defeated by its African colonies. Cuba remained afloat, despite every attempt to overthrow its government. No question that the Carnation Revolution of Portugal would not have taken place to overthrow the Estado Novo in 1974 without the wars of national liberation in Angola, Cape Verde, and Mozambique. No question that two decades later the apartheid regime of South Africa would not have fallen without the victory of the Angolan liberation forces with the Cubans against the South African

19 Ibid.

20 Philip Caputo, *A Rumor of War* (New York, 1977), xix.

21 Adrian Hastings, *Wiriyamu: My Lai in Mozambique* (New York: Orbis Books, 1974), 71, 75, 105.

regime in the 1987–88 battle of Cuito Cuanavale. Democracy in Portugal and in South Africa was taken by the gun. It was not given by liberalism. This narrative is now submerged. It has to be revived. Not just the sounds of the battlefield, but also the stories of the doctors and the technicians, of the revolutionary educational programs in Mozambique and Cape Verde, the attempt to build a new society out of the detritus of the colonial order. This was the revolutionary energy that is now forgotten.[22]

It was not forgotten due to the passage of time. A condition of amnesia was produced by the corporate media and the profession of history-writing, both of whom became stenographers of power. There was concerted effort by the West to undermine the entire dynamic of decolonization, from coups against the Ghanaian people (1966) to coups against the Chilean people (1973). Violence by the colonizer was slowly justified in humanitarian terms, with the West re-establishing itself as the architect of humanity who would now need to manage the violence of the native. The great decolonization process—whose highpoint was in the 1960s and 1970s—became the prelude to poverty and war that now wracks the former Third World. Beneath the paving stones in these colonized lands there is no beach. Beneath the paving stones, the corpses of freedom fighters.

22 Basil Davidson, *No Fist is Big Enough to Hide the Sky: The Liberation of Guinea-Bissau and Cape Verde, 1963–1974* (London: Zed Books, 2017); Edward George, *The Cuban Intervention in Angola, 1965–1991: From Che Guevara to Cuito Cuanavale* (Abingdon, U.K., New York: Routledge, 2005).

U.N. CHARTER

In 1945, the United Nations came into existence. At the meeting in San Francisco, a Charter was drafted which articulated the highest principles of statecraft and international relations. The U.N. Charter drew from the failed efforts of the League of Nations, whose own documents struggled to come to terms with the complexities of universal jurisdiction and the reality of a colonized world.

Old colonial masters liked to think that they were directed by God to bring peace and civilization to the world. That idea of the colonizer as peacemaker and lawgiver shuffled into the grand discourses of international law. Natives were fractious, unable to be governed by reason; they needed their masters to help them, to be their trustees. The League of Nations Covenant (1919) assembled the lands of the natives into "trusteeships," so that their masters could believe that their domination was sanctified by law. It was in Article 16 of the Covenant that the "peace loving nations"—namely, the imperialists—had the "obligation" to maintain peace and security.[23]

Japan's representative to the League of Nations meeting was Baron Makino Nobuaki. His speech at the Versailles conference—tinged with naivete—put forward a "proposal to abolish racial discrimination."[24] Nobuaki's brief was

[23] The Covenant of the League of Nations (Including Amendments adopted to December 1924), The Avalon Project, Lillian Goldman Law Library, Yale Law School, https://avalon.law.yale.edu/20th_century/leagcov.asp, accessed March 15, 2020.

[24] "Amendment of the Japanese Delegation for the Equality of All Nations," in *Papers Relating to the Foreign Relations of the United States, The Paris Peace Conference, 1919, Volume III*, Joseph V. Fuller, ed. (Washington, D.C.: United States Government Printing

narrow, as made clear by Foreign Minister Viscount Yasuya Uchida; this proposal would only apply to the members of the League of Nations, and not to the colonized territories. But even this principle was too much. Australia had officially adopted a White Australia Policy in 1901. Its Prime Minister William Morris Hughes would not tolerate such a proposal at the League. Both Britain and the United States of America agreed. The Japanese proposal fell by the wayside. Baron Nobuaki returned home furious; he was a patron of the ultra-nationalist groups whose role drove Japan toward its own imperial interlude.

On the ashes of Dresden and Hiroshima, the Allies fashioned the United Nations in 1945. Power was to be held in the five permanent members of the Security Council—France, China, United Kingdom, the U.S.S.R., and the United States. The U.N. Charter adopted the League of Nations' concern with how the "great powers" must be responsible for international security. In Article 39 of the Charter, the powers agreed that it would be the U.N. Security Council which would "determine the existence of any threat to the peace, breach of the peace, or act of aggression" in the world. In the Council, the five permanent members would have a veto over the overall decision-making; it was a Council of the five rather than of the 51 founding members of the United Nations. In Article 41, the Charter goes on that it is the Security Council that "may decide what measure not involving the use of armed force are to be employed to give effects to its decision." The United Nations said that these measures could include "complete or partial interruption of

Office, 1943), document 7, 289–91, https://history.state.gov/historicaldocuments/ frus1919Parisv03/d7, accessed March 15, 2020.

economic relations and of air, rail, sea, postal, telegraphic, radio, and other means of communication, and the severance of diplomatic relations."[25] This is the long form of the legal justification for sanctions.

If these did not work, Article 42 under Chapter VII allowed the "member states" to use armed force against sovereign nations. Some "member states" had more power than the others. One sought preponderant power. That was the United States.

It is important to recognize that the U.N. Charter provided the legal framework for lawless interventionism. The five permanent members of the U.N. Security Council, and not the almost two hundred states in the U.N. General Assembly, have the power to decide when and how to intervene against sovereign states.

From 1945 to 1989, the U.S.S.R. operated as an umbrella against the fully lawless usage of these U.N. loopholes, these mechanisms to offer the old colonial states a backdoor to continue their colonial wars in a modern form. The importance of this shield came within the first decade of the U.N. operations. The U.S.S.R. boycotted the Security Council because the United Nations did not replace the Nationalist Chinese delegate with the delegate from the People's Republic of China; during this period, the West weaponized the United Nations to authorize its intervention into South Korea against the communist forces in the north. The U.S.S.R. reversed its boycott as a consequence of this inability to veto the U.N. action. It returned to the United Nations. The first 56 vetoes in the U.N. Security Council were made by the U.S.S.R. The importance of the shield comes mainly on the anti-colonial, national liberation question. It was the U.S.S.R. that used

[25] U.N. Charter art. 39; U.N. Charter art. 41.

its veto to defend the process of national liberation from the struggles of the Palestinians to the struggles in South Rhodesia, from the South African freedom struggle to the liberation war in Vietnam.

EXPOSE THE UNITED STATES UNNECESSARILY

The United States has always hesitated before admitting its own colonial history. The Monroe Doctrine of 1823 merely said that the United States will defend the Americas from the Europeans, even though the implication—as the United States has always interpreted it—is that the Americas are the backyard of the United States alone. Even the U.S. role in the "Spanish-American" war is shrouded in the falsehood that the United States sent its troops in 1898 into Cuba, Guam, the Philippines, Puerto Rico, and Samoa to help liberate these lands from the Spanish empire. In fact, the United States absorbed these countries into its orbit, forcibly defeating the national liberation forces in each of these places. Cuba's revolutionaries were denied a role at the peace talks in Paris, and U.S. General William Shafter did not allow General Calixto Garcia to attend the Spanish surrender in Cuba. This was symbolic of the usurpation of the gains of that war by the United States. None of these former Spanish colonies were allowed to become independent; they were hastily absorbed into the expanding archipelago of U.S. power.

The main political leaders in the United States masked their imperialism by various forms of anti-imperialism. Albert Beveridge, the U.S. Senator for Indiana, wrote a tract with just this theme—*For the Greater Republic, Not for Imperialism* (1899). "Imperialism is not the word for our vast work," Beveridge wrote, because imperialism came with all the suggestions of domination and theft. What imperialism truly represents, he continued, is the "mighty movement and mission of our race."[26] What was that mission? The imperialist did not act to aggrandize himself, to steal wealth; he worked to bring civilization to the barbarians. This was an old trick—the mission of civilization as the objective of imperialism, when it was clear from all evidence that the objective was to plunder wealth and subordinate sovereignty.

This anxiety about being an imperialist power runs through the entire history of Washington's expansion. In 1962, the administration of U.S. President John F. Kennedy produced an Overseas Internal Defense Policy document. It is a clear statement of the class allegiance of the United States with the worst elements of countries in the Third World—despite the glamour of the Kennedy administration and its veneer of liberalism. This Policy document was being prepared by Kennedy's team just as 6,500 U.S. Marines landed in Thailand to "support that country during the threat of Communist pressure from outside," and just as Kennedy—after his failed attempt to overthrow the government in Cuba—pledged to "go all the way" against Vietnam's communist government. This 1962 document merely established in print what had already been written in blood: that the full force of the United States would be used to make sure that "developing nations evolve in a way that affords a congenial world environment for international cooperation and the growth of free institutions"; all this is verbiage for a simple motto: the U.S. government will make the world safe for the capitalist system whose major beneficiaries were transnational corporations (most of them

[26] Albert Beveridge, "For the Greater Republic, Not for Imperialism," Address at the Union League, Philadelphia, February 15, 1899.

based in the West). In fact, there is no need to annotate the Policy document. The United States, the authors write, has an "economic interest in assuring that the resources and markets of the less developed world remain available to us and to other Free World countries."[27]

Those Marines arrived in Thailand in July 1962. They had come to bolster the anti-communist militias and the Thai police—both trained by the CIA—in a war to weaken the communist Pathet Lao forces in nearby Laos and the Communist Party of Thailand, which began armed struggle in 1961. The United States sent in its premier former CIA diplomat John Peurifoy to oversee operations in Thailand, and to ensure that the military—led by Field Marshal Sarit Thanarat—came to power. Millions of dollars flowed out of the Kennedy administration to train the Thai Army and the Royal Lao Army in a project known as Ekarad. Theirs was a policy—as the U.S. embassy in Bangkok put it—of "covert harassment." It is what created the conditions for a clash with the Pathet Lao, the triggering of the SEATO pact, and then the arrival of U.S. troops—with the sound of U.S. aircraft overhead, threatening the wrath of napalm. Garment workers from factories that ringed Bangkok and college students moved in a radical direction; they, along with the insurgency at the fringes of the country, threatened the monarchy, the military, and the bourgeoisie. It was to crush them that the

[27] US Department of State, "U.S. Overseas Internal Defense Policy," in *Foreign Relations of the United States, 1961–1963, Volumes VII, VIII, IX, Arms Control; National Security Policy; Foreign Economic Policy, Microfiche Supplement*, Evans Gerakas, David W. Mabon, David S. Patterson et al., eds. (Washington, D.C.: United States Government Printing Office, 1997), document 279, https://history.state.gov/historicaldocuments/frus1961-63v07-09mSupp/d279, accessed March 15, 2020.

United States lent its full force, in return for which it got a subordinated ally and military bases—and it could ensure its economic interests remained alive and well.[28]

The intervention of the U.S. Marines—little known now as it was little discussed then—took place alongside the "covert harassment" provided by droves of U.S. advisors to the Thai and Laotian military forces. The United States whispered into the ears of the militaries of these regions, who were quite pleased to suspend any talk of democracy in the interests of stability; stability is a synonym for anti-communism. These militaries were not simply marionettes of U.S. power; they represented classes in their own societies that wanted to suppress workers and peasants to maintain both local oligarchic rule—from which they benefited—and international imperialism—from which the United States and its allies benefited.

It was impossible for the United States to admit that it was an imperialist power. The times were against that. In January 1962, Kennedy asked the CIA Deputy Director for Plans Richard Bissell to oversee Special Group (Counter-Insurgency). It was this group that produced the Overseas Internal Defense Policy document. Bissell was born in Hartford, Connecticut, in the home that was built by Mark Twain, one of the leaders of the Anti-Imperialist League that was set up to protest the U.S. war on the Philippines. Bissell went to Yale, and then the CIA; the men who joined him in this group were also well-read men from Harvard, Princeton,

28 Report, "Southeast Asia Situation Report," Joint Chiefs of Sta5 Director of Operations 23-63, June 6, 1962, file Top Secrets FE 5600-5699, Bureau of Far Eastern Affairs, Assistant Secretary of State for Far East Asia, Top Secret Files of the Regional Planning Adviser, Box 1, RG 59, USNA.

and Yale. They knew both their history and their current events. The Special Group emphasized covertness in its operations. U.S. power must be used through military action (asymmetrical wars), but also through the use of measures such as economic inducements and sanctions as well as support for local police and military forces (hybrid wars). "It is important," Bissell and his colleagues wrote, "for the U.S. to remain in the background, and where possible, to limit its support to training, advice, and material, lest it prejudice the local government effort and expose the U.S. unnecessarily to charges of intervention and colonialism."[29]

TOTAL WAR AND HYBRID WAR

As the lights went out in the U.S.S.R. and as the Third World Project surrendered before imperialist liberalization, a new era of intervention opened up. It is not as if intervention did not take place, that the Western intelligence services did not overthrow governments and the West did not invade countries. All that happened was that after the fall of the U.S.S.R. and the surrender of the Third World, the shield at the United Nations disappeared and the interventions from the West came fast and furiously.

It had been clear for several decades before 1989 that the United States had the most powerful military force in the world. The U.S. invasion of Panama in 1989 was a dress rehearsal for the new wars of the post-Cold War era. The United States fastened upon an old ally—Manuel Noriega—who had served the CIA faithfully for decades; this ally is now demonized as the worst rascal on the planet, with the media bleating out its approbation of his many terrible qualities.

[29] US Department of State, "U.S. Overseas Internal Defense Policy," 15.

Then, once the ideological terrain was set, the United States launched a massive invasion that began with aerial bombardment to pacify the recumbent security forces of the new enemy. The entire war was televised, with the visuals a warning to others not to stand against the United States, and a celebration for allies of the awesomeness of U.S. power. The U.N. General Assembly condemned the invasion as a "flagrant violation of international law."[30] The U.N. Security Council hastily put together a resolution against the invasion, but—without argument—France, the United Kingdom, and the United States vetoed it. There was no embarrassment at this extreme use of force.

On August 2, 1990, Iraq's armies invaded Kuwait—partly in retribution for an oil dispute, partly because Saddam Hussein wished to claim an unpaid debt from the Gulf Arabs for the war against Iran. The United States, through the Carter Doctrine, was obliged to protect Saudi Arabia, which borders Kuwait. The entire weight of the U.S. war machine descended on the Arabian Peninsula and in the waters of the Gulf. Under immense pressure from the United States, the United Nations passed resolution 661 (August 1990) which provides the template for sanctions regimes in our time. This resolution allowed the United Nations to enforce a medieval siege against the people of Iraq from its passage in 1990 until the United States invaded Iraq in 2003. The United States pressured the U.N. council members to adopt resolution 678 (November 1990) under Chapter VII—which allowed "member states" to use "all necessary means," including armed action against Iraq.[31] Cuba and Yemen were the only countries

[30] G.A. Res. 44/240 U.N. Doc. A/RES/44/240 (December 29, 1989), https://undocs.org/en/A/RES/44/240, accessed March 15, 2020.

[31] S.C. Res. 661 U.N. Doc. S/RES/661 (August 6, 1990), https://

to vote against this resolution, which gave the United States sanction from the United Nations to destroy Iraq. When the dust settled by March 1991, the United Nations sent a team into Iraq led by Under-Secretary General Martti Ahtisaari. It found that the U.S. bombardment had returned Iraq to a "pre-industrial age" and left it in a "near apocalyptic" state. Iraq—without adequate food and provisions—was near "imminent catastrophe," and could face "epidemic and famine if massive life-supporting needs are not rapidly met."[32] This did not move anyone. The U.N. resolutions came hard and fast, and Iraq's population suffered the destruction of civilization.

Sitting in one of the regime's palaces on February 24, 1991, Saddam Hussein and his closest advisors worried about the onslaught that was to come. The United States had been bombing Iraqi positions for the past month, and that day U.S. forces entered Kuwait. Hussein wondered why the U.S.S.R. had not intervened to prevent the escalation of the U.S. armies into the Gulf region. Already the Soviet Union had begun its descent into collapse, which it would do later that year. But in February the Iraqi leadership wondered about the silence from Moscow. Saddam's Culture Minister, Hamid Hammadi, put the point plainly. The United States had not intervened with such force because of Iraq's aggression, however egregious that was—after all, the Iraqis

digitallibrary.un.org/ record/94221?, accessed March 15, 2020; S.C. Res. 678 U.N. Doc. S/RES/678 (November 29, 1990), https://digitallibrary.un.org/record/102245?, accessed March 15, 2020.

32 Martti Ahtisaari, Under-Secretary General for Administration and Management, *Report to the Secretary-General on Humanitarian Needs in Kuwait and Iraq in the Immediate Post-Crisis Environment by a Mission to the Area*, U.N. Doc. S/22366 (March 20, 1991), 5, 13, www.un.org/Depts/oip/background/reports/s22366.pdf, accessed March 15, 2020.

believed that the U.S. ambassador to Iraq, April Glaspie, had given them the green light to invade Kuwait. Nor did the Iraqis believe that issue was simply Iraq's role in the Middle East—a problem that did worry the Gulf sheikhs but had not previously troubled Washington. The rush to war, Hammadi pointed out, was something other than this. "All these developments intend not only to destroy Iraq," he told the inner circle, "but to eliminate the role of the Soviet Union so the United States can control the fate of all humanity."[33]

Hammadi's assessment mirrored that of the U.S. government's own analysts. A policy group of the U.S. Defense Department—Team B—drafted a Defense Planning Guidance in 1990. "Our first objective," the Team—led by Dick Cheney—wrote:

> is to prevent the re-emergence of a new rival, either on the territory of the former Soviet Union or elsewhere, that poses a threat on the order of that posed by the Soviet Union. This is the dominant consideration and requires that we endeavor to prevent any hostile power from dominating a region whose resources would, under consolidated control, be sufficient to generate global power. Our strategy must now refocus on precluding the emergence of any potential future global competitor.[34]

This is what Hammadi told Hussein inside the palace as U.S. bombs dropped around them. It is what the Project

[33] Conflict Records Research Center, Record no. SH-SHTP-A-000-931, Transcript of conversation between Saddam Hussein and his inner circle, February 24, 1991, https://conflictrecords.files.wordpress.com/2011/09/sh-shtp-a-000-931_og.mp3, accessed March 15, 2020.

[34] "Excerpts from Pentagon's Plan 'Prevent the Re-emergence of a New Rival,'" *New York Times*, March 8, 1992.

for a New American Century had said in its *Rebuilding America's Defenses* a decade later, "American peace is to be maintained and expanded"; Pax Americana, another way of saying U.S. imperialism, "must have a secure foundation on unquestioned U.S. military pre-eminence."[35] It would be repeated in George W. Bush's 2002 *National Security Strategy of the United States of America* noted in familiar tones, "Our forces will be strong enough to dissuade potential adversaries from pursuing a military build-up in the hopes of surpassing, or equaling, the power of the United States."[36]

But asymmetrical war—the total war—has never been enough. It can win battles and destroy cities, but it does not win wars and infiltrate the mind and heart. To have "full spectrum dominance" over a society requires more than that—it requires a hybrid war that includes sabotage and economic blockades as well as cultural and media campaigns to undermine alternative theories of reality. The hybrid war is a combination of unconventional and conventional means using a range of state and non-state actors that run across the spectrum of social and political life. Part of this hybrid warfare is the battle over ideas, with the United States and its oligarchic allies smothering hostile countries by sabotage and economic blockades and then egging on the population to act in a "color revolution" against the government. Once the regime is changed, there is no political weight for the

[35] Thomas Donnelly, *Rebuilding America's Defenses: Strategy, Forces and Resources for a New Century* (Washington, D.C.: Project for the New American Century, September 2000), 4, https://web.archive.org/web/20061107194954/http://newamericancentury.org/RebuildingAmericasDefenses.pdf, accessed March 15, 2020.

[36] White House, *National Security Strategy of the United States of America* (Washington, D.C.: White House, 2002), 30, https://2009-2017.state.gov/documents/ organization/63562.pdf, accessed March 15, 2020.

people themselves to craft a new government which is more attuned to popular hopes. Instead, the cast of characters who people the new regime are old faces from the oligarchy and from various U.S. training programs.

Ordinary people in Latin America are not fooled by the language that comes from Washington. They are in fact horrified to see the return of men such as Elliott Abrams, a convicted criminal and friend of the brutal former dictator of Guatemala (Efraín Ríos Montt), to the front of this campaign to overthrow the government in Venezuela.

In Venezuela, the word "Chavista" has a resonance. It refers to those women and men who are loyal to Chávez and to the Bolivarian Revolution. It is not uncommon to see t-shirts with Chávez on them, his image ubiquitous on the walls. These are not people who have become rich or become powerful. They are part of a movement to chip away at hundreds of years of inequality. They remain poor, but now they have some resources to live without desperation.

So much needs to be changed, says Mariela Machado, a leader in the housing complex in Caracas, Venezuela, known as Kaikachi in the neighborhood of La Vega. We are poor. We have no resources. We have bad habits. We need time to develop our revolution. "Our revolution has to be done. It must happen. It is in process." A man nearby tells me that socialism is not a utopia. It is a difficult journey. The Chavistas mobilize almost weekly. They are on the streets to reaffirm their commitment to defend this difficult process.

The garrote of sanctions is tight. Imperialism will not relent, even as a global pandemic washes over Venezuela. What resources exist in the country, with Cuban, Chinese, and WHO help, will be mobilized to defend the humanity of the people. It is all that can be done. It is all that must be done. There is more humanity in each of these small voices than in the vaults of power and wealth.

CORONASHOCK AND THE HYBRID WAR AGAINST VENEZUELA

Ana Maldonado, Paola Estrada, Zoe PC, and Vijay Prashad

CoronaShock is a term that refers to how a virus struck the world with such gripping force; it refers to how the social order in the bourgeois state crumbled, while the social order in the socialist parts of the world appeared more resilient.

> But even the president of the United States
> sometimes must have to stand naked.
>
> —Bob Dylan, *It's Alright, Ma*, 1965

THE FOLLY OF HYBRID WAR

Swiftly moves the Coronavirus and COVID-19, dashing across continents, skipping over oceans, terrifying populations in every country. The numbers of those infected continue to rise, as do the numbers of those who have died. Hands are being washed, tests are being done, physical distance is being observed. It is unclear how devastating this pandemic will be or how long it will last.

On March 23, twelve days after the World Health Organization declared a global pandemic, the U.N. Secretary General António Guterres said, "The fury of the virus illustrates the folly of war. That is why today I am calling for an immediate global ceasefire in all corners of the world. It is time to put armed conflict on lockdown and focus together on the true fight of our lives."[37] Secretary General Guterres talked about silencing the guns, stopping the artillery, and ending the airstrikes. He did not refer to a specific conflict, leaving his plea to hang heavily in the air. After six weeks of deliberation and delay caused by Washington, in the first week of May, the United States government blocked a vote in the U.N. Security Council on a resolution that called for a global ceasefire.[38]

The United States blocked this resolution, but even this resolution did not turn its attention to the kind of war that the U.S. is prosecuting against Cuba, Iran, and Venezuela—among others. Instead, it has imposed a hybrid war. The U.S. military complex has advanced its hybrid war programme,[39]

[37] United Nations Secretary-General, "Transcript of the Secretary-General's virtual press encounter on the appeal for global ceasefire," March 23, 2020, https://www.un.org/sg/en/content/sg/press-encounter/2020-03-23/transcript-of-the-secretary-generals-virtual-press-encounter-the-appeal-for-global-ceasefire, accessed October 5, 2020.

[38] Julian Borger, "US blocks vote on U.N.'s bid for global ceasefire over reference to WHO," *The Guardian*, May 8, 2020, https://www.theguardian.com/world/2020/may/08/un-ceasefire-resolution-us-blocks-who, accessed October 5, 2020.

[39] "Vijay Prashad—Hybrid Wars and US Imperialism," The People's Forum NYC, https://www.youtube.com/watch?v=D-uxISFZbG8, accessed October 5, 2020.

which includes a range of techniques to undermine governments and political projects. These techniques include the mobilization of U.S. power over international institutions (such as the IMF, the World Bank, and the SWIFT wire service) in order to prevent governments from managing basic economic activity; the use of U.S. diplomatic power to isolate governments; the use of sanctions methods to prevent private companies from doing business with certain governments; the use of information warfare to render governments and political forces to be criminals or terrorists; and so on. This powerful complex of instruments is able—in the plain light of day—to destabilize governments and to justify regime change (for more on this, see the Tricontinental: Institute for Social Research dossier no. 17, *Venezuela and Hybrid Wars in Latin America*).[40]

During a pandemic, one would expect that all countries would collaborate in every way to mitigate the spread of the virus and its impact on human society. One would expect that a humanitarian crisis of this magnitude would provide the opportunity to end all inhumane economic sanctions and political blockades against certain countries. On March 24, the day after U.N. Secretary General Guterres's plea, U.N. High Commissioner for Human Rights Michelle Bachelet agreed that "at this crucial time, both for global public health reasons, and to support the rights and lives of millions of people in these countries, sectoral sanctions should be eased or suspended. In a context of [a] global pandemic, impeding medical efforts in one country heightens the risk for all

40 "Venezuela and Hybrid Wars in Latin America," Tricontinental: Institute for Social Research, dossier no. 17, June 3, 2019, https://www.thetricontinental.org/dossier-17-venezuela-and-hybrid-wars-in-latin-america/, accessed October 5, 2020.

of us."[41]

A few days later, Hilal Elver, the U.N. Special Rapporteur on the right to food, said that she was gratified to hear both Guterres and Bachelet call for an end to the sanctions regime. The problem, she indicated, lies with Washington: "The U.S., under the current administration, is very keen to continue the sanctions. Fortunately, some other countries are not. For instance, the European Union and many of the European countries are responding positively and easing sanctions during this time of the coronavirus. They are not completely lifting sanctions but interrupting them, and there are some communications going on, but not in the U.S., unfortunately."[42]

On May 6, three other U.N. Special Rapporteurs—Olivier De Schutter (on extreme poverty and human rights), Léo Heller (on human rights to safe drinking water and sanitation), and Koumbou Boly Barry (on the right to education)—said that "in light of the coronavirus pandemic, the United States should immediately lift blanket sanctions, which are having a severe impact on the human rights of the Venezuelan people."[43] Nevertheless, the Trump administration has brushed aside all concern and continued

[41] "Ease sanctions against countries fighting COVID-19: U.N. human rights chief," U.N. News, March 24, 2020, https://news.un.org/en/story/2020/03/1060092, accessed October 5, 2020.

[42] "To Lift or Not to Lift: Will Covid-19 Shake Up Sanctions?," UN-Scripted, Ep. 20, https://soundcloud.com/user-936032402/ep20-pandemic-sanctions-shake-up, accessed October 5, 2020.

[43] "Venezuela must offer concrete steps to end humanitarian crisis, say UN experts," Office of the High Commissioner for Human Rights, May 6, 2020, https://www.ohchr.org/EN/NewsEvents/Pages/DisplayNews.aspx?NewsID=25867&LangID=E, accessed October 5, 2020.

with its agenda of hybrid war towards regime change.

HABITS OF REGIME CHANGE

As COVID-19 moved toward South America, the U.S. government increased pressure on the Venezuelan government. In February 2020 at the Munich Security Conference, U.S. Secretary of State Mike Pompeo said that the U.S. seeks to "oust Maduro."[44] The following month, on March 12, the U.S. tightened sanctions against Venezuela,[45] and then the U.S. Treasury Department put pressure on the International Monetary Fund not to allow Venezuela access to emergency funds to tackle the global pandemic.[46] None of this worked. Despite the lack of support from the IMF, the Venezuelan government mobilized the people to break the chain of infection, with international assistance from China, Cuba, and Russia, as well as the World Health Organization.

At this point, the U.S. government shifted its focus. It suggested that President Nicolás Maduro and his senior leadership are involved in narco-trafficking. No evidence was offered for this hallucinatory claim, although there is

44 "The West Is Winning," Speech by Mike Pompeo, Secretary of State, US, at the Munich Security Conference, Munich, Germany, February 15, 2020, https://www.state.gov/the-west-is-winning/, accessed October 5, 2020.

45 Lara Jakes, "U.S. Imposes Sanctions on Russian Oil Company Supporting Venezuela's Leader," *New York Times*, February 18, 2020, https://www.nytimes.com/2020/02/18/world/americas/venezuela-russia-sanctions-trump.html, accessed October 5, 2020.

46 Ana Maldonado, Paola Estrada, Vijay Prashad, Zoe PC, "IMF Refuses Aid to Venezuela In the Midst of the Coronavirus Crisis," *Peoples Dispatch*, March 19, 2020, https://peoplesdispatch.org/2020/03/19/imf-refuses-aid-to-venezuela-in-the-midst-of-the-coronavirus-crisis/, accessed October 5, 2020.

substantial evidence of the culpability of senior Colombian politicians in the drug trade. U.S. President Donald Trump authorized a naval detachment to sit off the coast of Venezuela,[47] threaten its government, and intimidate its population. On April 30, to increase pressure on Venezuela, the Trump administration activated parts of the Selected Reserve of the Armed Forces to assist the U.S. armed forces in a mission named "Enhanced Department of Defense Counternarcotic Operation in the Western Hemisphere."[48] All signs point to mischief by the U.S. and its Colombian allies against the Venezuelan people.

The United States government has been entirely candid about its goal to overthrow the Venezuelan government, currently led by President Maduro, and to reverse the Bolivarian Revolution. In August 2017, Trump spoke openly about the "military option"[49] at the same time as the United States, Canada, Colombia, and a list of other countries governed by the far right and subordinated to Washington formed the Lima Group. The Lima Group tried to maintain a liberal patina around their objective, stating in their

47 Remarks by President Trump, Vice President Pence, and Members of the Coronavirus Task Force in Press Briefing, April 1, 2020, https://www.whitehouse.gov/briefings-statements/remarks-president-trump-vice-president-pence-members-coronavirus-task-force-press-briefing-16/, accessed October 5, 2020.

48 Donald Trump's Executive Order on Ordering the Selected Reserve of the Armed Forces to Active Duty, April 30, 2020, https://www.whitehouse.gov/presidential-actions/executive-order-ordering-selected-reserve-armed-forces-active-duty/, accessed October 5, 2020.

49 "Trump Alarms Venezuela With Talk of a 'Military Option,'" *New York Times*, August 12, 2017, https://www.nytimes.com/2017/08/12/world/americas/trump-venezuela-military.html, accessed October 5, 2020.

declaration that they wished to "facilitat[e] . . . the restoration of the rule of law and constitutional and democratic order in Venezuela."[50] Trump ripped aside the fig leaf of this kind of liberal language and interpreted the phrase "restoration of democratic order" quite rightly as a call for a military coup or an armed intervention to overthrow the government.

In January 2019, the United States government deepened its hybrid war with a clever diplomatic manoeuvre. It declared that Juan Guaidó, an insignificant politician, was the president of Venezuela and turned over substantial Venezuelan assets outside the country to him. An attempted uprising led by Guaidó and the far-right in Venezuela to oust Maduro and claim power failed to materialize, and Guaidó found himself with more friends in Washington, D.C. and amongst Colombia's oligarchy than at home in Venezuela. However, this failed attempt to overthrow the Venezuelan government did not deter the United States. In fact, the failure deepened U.S. intervention in the region.

In May 2019, Senator Lindsey Graham took to the pages of the *Wall Street Journal* to make the case that the "U.S. must be willing to intervene in Venezuela the way we did in Grenada."[51] In 1983, the U.S. marines landed in Grenada to overthrow the legitimate government and to uproot the New Jewel Movement. Should certain measures not be taken, Senator Graham wrote that the United States "should move

[50] "Lima Group Declaration," Ministry of Foreign Affairs, International Trade and Worship, Argentina, September 23, 2019, https://www.cancilleria.gob.ar/en/announcements/news/lima-group-declaration-3, accessed October 5, 2020.

[51] Lindsey Graham, "Match Words With Actions in Venezuela, Mr. President," *Wall Street Journal*, May 22, 2019, https://www.wsj.com/articles/match-words-with-actions-in-venezuela-mr-president-11558565556, accessed October 5, 2020.

military assets to the region." The United States attempted to create a phalanx of allies in the Brazilian and Colombian militaries to prepare for an invasion of Venezuela. Fortunately, at the Lima Group meeting in February 2019, Brazil's vice president Hamilton Mourão told the press that Brazil would not allow the U.S. to use its territory for a military intervention into Venezuela.[52] The plans of a full-scale invasion had to be put on hold.

COLLECTIVE PUNISHMENT

On March 10, Venezuela's Foreign Minister Jorge Arreaza told us that the "illegal and unilateral coercive measures that the United States has imposed on Venezuela are a form of collective punishment." The use of the phrase "collective punishment" is significant; under the 1949 Geneva Convention, any policy that inflicts damage on an entire population is a war crime. The U.S. policy, Arreaza told us, has "resulted in difficulties for the timely acquisition of medicines."

On paper, the unilateral U.S. sanctions say that medical supplies are exempt. But this is an illusion. On March 26, eleven U.S. Senators sent a letter to U.S. Secretary of State Mike Pompeo and U.S. Treasury Secretary Steve Mnuchin to say: "We understand that the administration has stated that humanitarian and medical needs are exempt from U.S. sanctions, but our sanctions regime is so broad that medical suppliers and relief organizations simply steer clear of doing

[52] "Brasil não permitirá que EUA usem território para invadir," *Valor Econômico*, February 25, 2019, https://valor.globo.com/mundo/noticia/2019/02/25/brasil-nao-permitira-que-eua-usem-territorio-para-invadir-venezuela.ghtml, accessed October 5, 2020.

business in Iran and Venezuela in fear of accidentally getting caught up in the U.S. sanctions web."[53] Neither Venezuela nor Iran can easily buy medical supplies, nor can they easily transport them into their countries, nor can they use them in their largely public sector health systems. The embargo against these countries—even more so in this time of COVID-19—is not only a war crime by the standards of the Geneva Convention (1949); it is also a crime against humanity as defined by the United Nations International Law Commission (1947).

In 2017, Trump enacted tight restrictions on Venezuela's ability to access financial markets. Two years later, the U.S. government blacklisted Venezuela's Central Bank and put a general embargo on Venezuelan state institutions. If any firm trades with Venezuela's public sector, it could face secondary sanctions. The U.S. Congress passed the Countering America's Adversaries Through Sanctions Act (CAATSA) in 2017, which tightened sanctions against Iran, Russia, and North Korea. The next year, Trump imposed a raft of new sanctions against Iran, which suffocated the country's economy. Once more, access to the world banking system and threats to companies that traded with Iran made it almost impossible for Iran to do business with the world. In particular, the U.S. government made it clear that any business with the public sector of Iran and Venezuela was forbidden. The health infrastructure that provides for the mass of the populations in both Iran and Venezuela is run by the state, which means

53 "Murphy Organizes Senate Effort to Call for Ease of U.S. Sanctions Hindering Response to COVID-19," US Senate, March 26, 2020, https://www.murphy.senate.gov/newsroom/press-releases/-murphy-organizes-senate-effort-to-call-for-ease-of-us-sanctions-hindering-response-to-covid-19, accessed October 5, 2020.

it faces disproportionate difficulty in accessing equipment and supplies, including testing kits and medicines.

Venezuela and Iran have relied on the World Health Organization (WHO) to obtain medicines and tests. Nonetheless, the WHO faces its own challenges with sanctions, particularly when it comes to transportation. These harsh sanctions forced transportation companies to reconsider servicing both Iran and Venezuela. Some airlines stopped flying there, and many shipping companies decided not to anger Washington. When the WHO tried to get testing kits for COVID-19 from the United Arab Emirates (UAE) into Iran, it faced difficulty "due to flight restrictions," as the WHO's Christoph Hamelmann put it.[54] The UAE sent the equipment via a military transport plane.

Likewise, Arreaza told us, Venezuela has "received solidarity from governments of countries such as China and Cuba." In late February, a team from the Red Cross Society of China arrived in Tehran to exchange information with the Iranian Red Crescent and with WHO officials. China has also donated testing kits and supplies. The sanctions, Chinese officials told us, should be of no consequence during a humanitarian crisis such as this; they are not going to honor them.

Meanwhile, the Iranians developed an app to help their population during the COVID-19 outbreak. Google decided to remove it from its app store, a consequence of the U.S. sanctions.

What kind of moral fibre holds together an international system where a handful of countries can act in a way that

[54] Christoph Hamelmann, Twitter post, February 28, 2020, https://twitter.com/cahamelmann/status/1233348062136938497, accessed October 5, 2020.

goes against all the highest aspirations of humanity? When the United States continues its embargoes against thirty-nine countries—but with greater intensity against Cuba, Iran, and Venezuela—when there is a global pandemic afoot, what does this say about the nature of power and authority in our world? Sensitive people should be offended by such behavior, its mean-spiritedness evident in the unnatural deaths that it provokes.

When then-U.S. Secretary of State Madeleine Albright was asked in 1996 about the half million Iraqi children who died because of U.S. sanctions, she said that those deaths were "a price worth paying." They were certainly not a price that the Iraqis wanted to pay, nor now the Iranians or the Venezuelans, or indeed most of humankind.

THE IMF TAKES ORDERS FROM THE U.S. TREASURY

On March 16, 2020, the chief of the International Monetary Fund (IMF) Kristalina Georgieva wrote a blog post on the Fund's website; it represents the kind of generosity necessary in the midst of a global pandemic. "The IMF stands ready to mobilize its $1 trillion lending capacity to help our membership," she wrote.[55] Countries with "urgent balance-of-payments needs" could be helped by the IMF's "flexible and rapid-disbursing emergency response toolkit." Through these mechanisms, and against its own history of structural adjustment conditions, the IMF said that it could provide $50 billion to developing countries and $10 billion to low-income countries at a zero-interest rate—without the usual

[55] Kristalina Georgieva, "Policy Action for a Healthy Global Economy," IMFBlog, March 16, 2020, https://blogs.imf.org/2020/03/16/policy-action-for-a-healthy-global-economy/, accessed October 5, 2020.

strings attached.

The day before Georgieva made this public statement, Venezuela's foreign ministry sent a letter to the IMF asking for funds to finance the government's "detection and response systems" for its efforts against the coronavirus. In the letter, President Nicolás Maduro wrote that his government is "executing different highly comprehensive, strict and exhaustive control measures . . . to protect the Venezuelan people."[56] These measures require funding, which is why the government is "turning to your honorable [organization] to request your evaluation about the possibility of granting Venezuela a financing facility of USD 5,000 million [5 billion] from the emergency fund of the Rapid Financing Instrument (RFI), resources that will contribute significantly to strengthen our detection and response systems."

Georgieva's policy to provide special assistance to countries should have been enough for the IMF to provide the assistance that the Venezuelan government had requested. But, very quickly, the Fund declined the request from Venezuela.

It is important to underline the fact that the IMF made this denial at a time when the coronavirus had begun to spread in Venezuela. On March 15, the day that Venezuelan President Nicolás Maduro's government sent the letter to the IMF, Maduro also met with senior government officials in Caracas. The state-owned Venezuelan pharmaceutical body (CIFAR) and the Venezuelan medical equipment companies said that they would be able to increase the production of machines and medicines to stem the crisis; but, they said, they would need key raw materials that have to be imported.

[56] Jorge Arreaza M, Twitter post, March 18, 2020, https://twitter.com/jaarreaza/status/1240035272601059328, accessed October 5, 2020.

The Venezuelan government went to the IMF in order to be able to pay for these imports. The denial of the loan directly impacted the Venezuelan health apparatus and impeded Venezuela from properly tackling the coronavirus pandemic.

"This is the most dire situation we have ever faced," said President Maduro as he put new measures in place. The Venezuelan government imposed an indefinite national quarantine and has implemented processes to distribute food and key supplies, building on the local self-government (communes) that developed with the Bolivarian Revolution. All of the institutions of the state are now involved in doing their part to help "flatten the curve" and "break the chain" of contagion. But, because of the IMF loan denial, the country has had a harder time producing testing kits, respirators, and key medicines for those infected with the virus.

Venezuela is a founding member of the IMF. It has, despite being an oil-rich state, come to the IMF several times for various forms of assistance. The cycle of IMF interventions in Venezuela in the 1980s and early 1990s led to an uprising in 1989 that delegitimized the Venezuelan elite; it was on the back of the popular protests against the IMF that Hugo Chávez built the coalition that propelled him to office in 1998 and that started the Bolivarian Revolution in 1999. By 2007, Venezuela paid off its outstanding debts to both the IMF and the World Bank; the country cut its ties to these institutions, hoping to build a Bank of the South—rooted in Latin America—as an alternative. But before this Bank could be set up, a round of crises struck Latin America, forced by a fall in commodity prices from 2014-15.

Venezuela's economy relies upon foreign oil exports to generate the revenue necessary to import goods. With the fall in oil prices between 2014 and 2018 came a directed attack on Venezuela by the United States, who imposed a new round of unilateral sanctions. These sanctions prevented oil companies and transportation firms from doing business with Venezuela; international banks seized Venezuela's holdings in their vaults (including $1.2 billion in gold in the Bank of England) and stopped doing business with Venezuela. This sanctions regime, tightened further by Donald Trump's administration, deeply hurt Venezuela's ability to sell its oil and buy products, including supplies for its state health sector.

In January 2019, after the U.S. supported Guaidó's attempt to usurp power, U.S. banks hastily seized the Venezuelan state assets that they held and turned them over to the self-proclaimed president. Then, in a startling move, the IMF said that the Venezuelan government would no longer be allowed to use its $400 million in special drawing rights (SDRs), the currency of the IMF. It said that it had taken this action because of the political uncertainty in Venezuela. In other words, because of the attempted coup—which failed—the IMF said that it would not "take sides" in Venezuela; by not "taking sides," the IMF refused to allow the government of Venezuela to access its own funds. Strikingly, Guaidó's adviser Ricardo Hausmann, a former IMF development committee chair and Guaidó's representative at the Inter-American Development Bank, said at that time that he expected that when the regime change occurs, the money will be available to the new government. This is the IMF directly interfering in Venezuelan politics.

Neither at that time nor now has the IMF denied that the government of Nicolás Maduro is the legitimate government in Venezuela. The IMF continues to acknowledge on its website that the representative of Venezuela in the IMF is

Simón Alejandro Zerpa Delgado, the minister of finance in Maduro's government. One of the reasons why this is so is that Guaidó could not prove that he had the support of most of the member states of the IMF. Since Guaidó could not prove his standing, the IMF—again, extraordinarily—has instead denied the Maduro government its legitimate right to its own funds and to borrow against facilities provided by the Fund to its members.

Normally, the IMF takes time when it gets a request for funds. The request must be studied by the analysts, who look at the situation in the country and see whether the request is legitimate. In this case, the IMF responded immediately. It said no.

A spokesperson for the Fund, Raphael Anspach, would not answer specific questions about this denial; in 2019, he had been similarly cautious about saying anything about the denial of access to the $400 million in SDRs. This time, Anspach sent us a formal statement that the IMF had released to the media. The statement said that, while the IMF sympathizes with the predicament of the Venezuelan people, "it is not in a position to consider this request." Why is this so? Because, the IMF says, its "engagement with member countries is predicated on official government recognition by the international community." "There is," the statement says, "no clarity on recognition at this time."

But there is clarity. The IMF listed the Venezuelan minister of finance on its website at least until mid-March. The United Nations continues to recognize the Venezuelan government, led by President Nicolás Maduro. That should be the official standard for the IMF to make its determination. But it is not. It is taking dictation from the U.S. government. In April 2019, U.S. Vice President Mike Pence went to the

U.N. Security Council, where he said that the U.N. should accept Juan Guaidó as the legitimate president of Venezuela; he turned to the Venezuelan ambassador to the U.N., Samuel Moncada Acosta, and said, "You shouldn't be here." This is a moment of great symbolism, the United States acting as if the U.N. is its home and that it can invite and uninvite whomsoever it wants. The IMF denial of the $5 billion request from Venezuela follows Pence's sentiment. It is a violation of the spirit of international cooperation that is at the heart of the U.N. Charter.

There are signs of weakness in the U.S. position. On December 18, 2019, the United Nations General Assembly adopted—without a vote—a resolution that accepted the credentials of the diplomats appointed by Maduro's government.[57] The fact that there was no vote taken reveals that the United States does not want to reveal in plain sight the minority support in the world for its position of isolating the government of Venezuela. The U.S. would rather forego a vote in the interest of fabricating and upholding a smoke and mirrors narrative allegedly held by the "international community" than allow the actual international community to vote openly and show that it accepts the Maduro government as the legitimate government of Venezuela.

THE HALLUCINATORY ACCUSATIONS

57 "General Assembly Adopts 26 Legal Committee Texts without Vote, Reaffirming Role of International Law in Promoting Peace, Security, Sustainable Development," U.N. General Assembly, Plenary, 74th Session, 51st Meeting, December 18, 2019, https://www.un.org/press/en/2019/ga12232.doc.htm, accessed October 5, 2020.

OF NARCO-TRAFFICKING

At a press conference on March 26, it was almost comical how little evidence the U.S. Department of Justice provided when it indicted Venezuela's President Nicolás Maduro and several of the leaders of his government of narco-trafficking.[58] The U.S. offered $15 million for the arrest of Maduro and $10 million for the others. Maduro, U.S. Attorney Geoffrey Berman said dramatically, "very deliberately deployed cocaine as a weapon." Evidence for this? Not presented at all. An indictment is not a verdict of guilt, merely a note—in this case—prepared by the U.S. government against an adversary; there is nothing in the indictment that proves the case that any of the individuals mentioned in it have anything to do with narcotics smuggling. It was apparent from the press conference at the U.S. Department of Justice that this was political theatre, an attempt to further delegitimize Maduro's government.[59]

It is surreal that the United States—during the COVID-19 global pandemic—chooses to put its efforts into this ridiculous, evidence-free indictment against Maduro and other members of the government. Already, there is pressure on the United States to lift the sanctions not only against Venezuela but also against Iran (even *The New York*

[58] "Attorney General Barr and DOJ Officials Announce Significant Law Enforcement Actions Relating to International Narco-Terrorism," US Department of Justice, video, https://www.justice.gov/opa/video/attorney-general-barr-and-doj-officials-announce-significant-law-enforcement-actions, accessed October 5, 2020.

[59] Leonardo Flores, "Trump's narcoterrorism indictment of Maduro already backfires," *Peoples Dispatch*, March 28, 2020, https://peoplesdispatch.org/2020/03/28/trumps-narcoterrorism-indictment-of-maduro-already-backfires/, accessed October 5, 2020.

Times came out on March 25 to call for an end to sanctions on Iran[60]). The World Health Organization has made it clear that this is just not the time to hamper the ability of countries to get precious supplies in to tackle the pandemic. Out of desperation, the U.S. tried to change the conversation—no longer about COVID-19 and sanctions, but about narco-terrorism.

When asked about these indictments during the COVID-19 pandemic, U.S. Attorney General William Barr tried to say that the fault lay not in Washington but in Caracas. He said, absent any evidence, that Venezuela is blocking aid from coming into the country. Nothing could be further from the truth, since Venezuela has welcomed medical supplies and medical personnel from China, Cuba, and Russia, as well as from the WHO. In fact, the WHO has pressed the U.S. to allow it freer rein to bring goods into the country—a request that the U.S. has not allowed. Barr can so easily say the very opposite of truth because none of the media outlets at the press conference would challenge him based on matters that are clearly in the public record.

In 1989, the U.S. used the accusation of narco-trafficking—specifically cocaine trafficking—to taint the reputation of its former asset, then-president of Panama Manuel Noriega. Based on this accusation[61] and an indictment in Florida, the U.S. eventually invaded the country, seized Noriega, planted Washington's puppet in Panama City, and threw Noriega into a Florida prison. The shadow of how the U.S. dealt with

---

60 "This Coronavirus Crisis Is the Time to Ease Sanctions on Iran," *New York Times*, March 25, 2020, https://www.nytimes.com/2020/03/25/opinion/iran-sanctions-covid.html, accessed October 5, 2020.

61 See *The Panama Deception*, 1992, https://topdocumentaryfilms.com/the-panama-deception/, accessed October 5, 2020.

Noriega hangs over Caracas.[62]

The bounty on the heads of Maduro and his leadership suggests that the U.S. government has essentially put a mafia-type hit out on these Venezuelans. This is a very dangerous move by the United States. It essentially gives gangsters a green light to attempt assassination inside Venezuela. The refusal to allow Maduro to travel outside of Venezuela is a violation of a series of international conventions that promote diplomacy over belligerence. But, given the lawless way that the U.S. has formulated its regime change strategy against Venezuela—and throughout history—it is unlikely that anyone is going to criticize this move.

A few hours before the announcement in Washington, word began to spread that the United States was going to place Venezuela's government on the "state sponsor of terrorism" list—the very highest condemnation of a government.[63] But they had to pause. And the pause itself came for absurd reasons. If the U.S. government accused Maduro's government of being a "state sponsor of terrorism," then it would be tacitly acknowledging that the Maduro government is indeed the government of Venezuela. Since January 2019, one of the attempts at destabilization had been to deny that Maduro's government is the legitimate government of Venezuela, indeed, to deny that it is any kind of government.

62 Dave DeCamp, "William Barr Greenlit Bush's Invasion of Panama, Is Venezuela Next?" *Antiwar*, March 30, 2020, https://original.antiwar.com/dave_decamp/2020/03/29/william-barr-greenlit-bushs-invasion-of-panama-is-venezuela-next/, accessed October 5, 2020.

63 Kay Guerrero, Evan Perez and David Shortell, "Trump administration targets Venezuela's President and other top officials," *CNN*, March 26, 2020, https://edition.cnn.com/2020/03/26/politics/venezuela-trump-administration-terrorism/index.html, accessed October 5, 2020.

It would be impossible to say that the Maduro government is a "state sponsor of terrorism" without acknowledging that it is the government of Venezuela. So, the United States had to stay its hand, caught out by its own logic.

The statement released by the U.S. Department of Justice reads like a thriller, and the lack of evidence lends it to comparison with fiction. It lists names and accusations, makes constant references to "narco-terrorism," and claims that the Venezuelan government wants to "flood" the United States with cocaine.[64] It would take a superhuman effort of blindness to believe this baseless ranting and raving. But the problem is that the people of Venezuela must take this seriously, since it is a deepening of the United States government's belligerence. The people of Venezuela are aware of the dangers of a Panama-type situation. It's hard to blame them. This is the track record of the United States government.

The comparison to a Panama-type situation cannot be written off as paranoia. On April's Fools Day, Trump gave a press conference in which he announced a new "counter-narcotics effort" by U.S. Southern Command.[65] "We're deploying additional Navy destroyers, combat ships,

64 "Nicolás Maduro Moros and 14 Current and Former Venezuelan Officials Charged with Narco-Terrorism, Corruption, Drug Trafficking and Other Criminal Charges," US Department of Justice, March 26, 2020, https://www.justice.gov/opa/pr/nicol-s-maduro-moros-and-14-current-and-former-venezuelan-officials-charged-narco-terrorism, accessed October 5, 2020.

65 Remarks by President Trump, Vice President Pence, and Members of the Coronavirus Task Force in Press Briefing, April 1, 2020, https://www.whitehouse.gov/briefings-statements/remarks-president-trump-vice-president-pence-members-coronavirus-task-force-press-briefing-16/, accessed October 5, 2020.

aircrafts and helicopters; Coast Guard cutters; and Air Force surveillance aircraft, doubling our capabilities in the region," he said. The point of this mission—which will be joined by other countries—is to "increase surveillance, disruption, and seizures of drug shipments." "We must not let the drug cartels exploit the pandemic to threaten American lives," he added.

Coming less than a week after the U.S. indictment, it became clear that the point is not actually to disrupt the cocaine trade, but to put pressure on Venezuela. No evidence was provided during the Department of Justice press conference when the United States charged Maduro with narco-trafficking, and no evidence was presented at Trump's press conference when he announced that a naval carrier group would enter the Caribbean. There was no evidence presented at either high-profile event, because no evidence is either available or necessary. It is not available because even the U.S. government's own agencies say that Venezuela is neither the originator of narcotics nor the trafficker of narcotics; it is not necessary because the United States has consistently used its position to invent increasingly hallucinatory stories about the Venezuelan government in order to delegitimize and overthrow it.

In December 2019, the U.S. Drug Enforcement Agency (DEA) released its "National Drug Threat Assessment."[66] This study offers the most detailed look at the movement of drugs into the United States. At several points in the study, the DEA says that Colombia is the "primary source for cocaine

[66] *2019 National Drug Threat Assessment*, US Department of Justice, Drug Enforcement Administration, December 2019, https://www.dea.gov/sites/default/files/2020-01/2019-NDTA-final-01-14-2020_Low_Web-DIR-007-20_2019.pdf, accessed October 5, 2020.

seized in the United States." According to the DEA's Cocaine Signature Program, in 2018 "approximately 90 percent of cocaine samples tested were of Colombian origin, six percent were of Peruvian origin, and four percent were of unknown origin." As far as the U.S. government's own drug agency is concerned, there is no cocaine or any other narcotic that comes from Venezuela.

Both at the U.S. Department of Justice press conference and at Trump's press conference, maps were shown that indicated cocaine traffic from Venezuela to the United States. This is simply not true, based on the information from the U.S. DEA: "The majority of the cocaine and heroin produced and exported by Colombian TCOs [Transnational Criminal Organizations] to the United States is transported through Central America and Mexico," write the DEA officials in their 2019 report. However, there are suggestions in the report that Colombian narco-traffickers sometimes "store large quantities of cocaine in remote areas of Venezuela and Ecuador until maritime or aerial transportation can be secured."

It is important to recognize that the cocaine and heroin are hidden in "remote areas" of Colombia's neighbors, with Colombia being the focus of the entire drug trade. At no point in the entire 146-page DEA document, and in documents from previous years, do the U.S. drug officials make any statement that implicates the Venezuelan government in either the production, storage, or transportation of the cocaine and heroin. The only time Venezuela enters the picture is when Colombian narco-traffickers hide their cocaine and heroin in "remote areas" of Venezuela before they traffic them into Central America and Mexico and then onwards to the United States.

There is significant evidence, however—as presented by the Colombian journalist Gonzalo Guillén in *La Nueva Prensa* on March 3, 2020—that Colombia's president Iván Duque and his patron, the former president Álvaro Uribe, had close ties with the narco-trafficker José Guillermo Hernández Aponte, alias Ñeñé.[67] The previous day, Duque was in the Oval Office as Trump chided him for not doing enough to eradicate cocaine production in Colombia. "Well, you're going to have to spray," Trump told Duque. "If you don't spray, you're not going to get rid of them. So, you have to spray, with regard to the drugs in Colombia."[68]

Trump was talking about glyphosate-based fumigation, which the government of Colombia halted in 2015 because the WHO said that such sprays caused cancer. Despite this, Duque said that he will restart spraying. There was no mention of the accusations that Duque himself is linked to the narco-traffickers; since he is pliant towards Washington, his own alleged crimes do not amount to much. Duque's patron Uribe, the former Colombian president and current Senate member, is currently implicated in more than 270 legal cases in Colombia with charges including illegal wiretapping, organized crime, selective assassinations, and

[67] "Interceptaciones al narcotraficante ´Ñeñe´ Hernández destapan compra de votos para Duque por orden de Uribe," *La Nueva Pensa*, March 3, 2020, https://www.lanuevaprensa.com.co/component/k2/interceptaciones-al-narcotraficante-nene-hernandez-destapan-compra-de-votos-para-duque-por-orden-de-uribe, accessed October 5, 2020.

[68] Remarks by President Trump and President Duque of Colombia Before Bilateral Meeting, March 2, 2020, https://www.whitehouse.gov/briefings-statements/remarks-president-trump-president-duque-colombia-bilateral-meeting-2/, accessed October 5, 2020.

forced disappearances.[69] Uribe and members of his family have proven links with the paramilitary group *Bloque Metro* ("Metro Block") of Antioquia, which was responsible for thousands of assassinations of Colombian civilians and was deeply involved in the narco-trafficking.

Strangely, in that press conference, both Trump and Duque talked about Venezuela, but neither of them mentioned drugs or narco-trafficking. It was all about regime change.

On March 31, U.S. Secretary of State Mike Pompeo announced that Venezuela must have a transitional government; this itself is bizarre because Pompeo is neither Venezuelan nor a United Nations official, and yet he felt emboldened to speak for the Venezuelan people. His plan, "Democratic Transition Framework for Venezuela," called upon President Maduro to resign and for Washington's favored replacement Juan Guaidó to continue his imaginary claim to power. Members of the four main parties, including Maduro's Socialist Party, would form a council and be led by an "interim president." If this plan is accepted, Washington would lift its unilateral coercive sanctions that it had imposed from 2014.

The previous weekend, Guaidó announced on Twitter that Venezuela needed an "emergency government" that had the participation of all parties and would govern until new elections could be held. After Pompeo's announcement, Guaidó took credit for it and thanked Pompeo publicly.

69 "'Narcopols': Medellín Cartel 'Financed' Senate Campaign of Former President Álvaro Uribe, Colombian Senators Told U.S. Embassy," National Security Archive, Briefing Book no. 631, https://nsarchive.gwu.edu/briefing-book/colombia/2018-05-25/narcopols-medellin-cartel-financed-senate-campaign-former, accessed October 5, 2020.

Other far-right politicians, such as Leopoldo López, Carlos Vecchio, and Julio Borges, saluted Pompeo's plan and thanked the United States for backing Guaidó's "emergency government."[70] When she heard that gunboats were coming towards the Venezuelan coast, Maria Corina Machado of the Vente Venezuela Party tweeted, "That's the way to build a credible threat."[71] It is credible because the gunboats have done this before.

The Organization of American States (OAS), which behaved[72] as the long-arm of the U.S. State Department during the coup against the government of Evo Morales in Bolivia last November, joined in the chorus begun by Pompeo and Guaidó.[73] In a statement, the OAS declared that it "considers that the plan presented constitutes a valid proposal for a path to end the usurping dictatorship and restore democracy in the country."[74]

70 Carlos Vecchio, Twitter post, April 1, 2020, https://twitter.com/carlosvecchio/status/1245119783370178560?s=20, accessed October 5, 2020.

71 María Corina Machado, Twitter post, April 2, 2020, https://twitter.com/MariaCorinaYA/status/1245470886397915143, accessed October 5, 2020.

72 Vijay Prashad and Alejandro Bejarano, "Elon Musk Is Acting Like a Neo-Conquistador for South America's Lithium," *Counterpunch*, March 11, 2020, https://www.counterpunch.org/2020/03/11/elon-musk-is-acting-like-a-neo-conquistador-for-south-americas-lithium/, accessed October 5, 2020.

73 "What Is Happening in Bolivia Regarding the 3 May Elections?" Tricontinental: Institute for Social Research, February 7, 2020, https://www.thetricontinental.org/bolivia/, accessed October 5, 2020.

74 Statement from the OAS General Secretariat on the Situation in Venezuela, Organization of American States, March 31, 2020, https://www.oas.org/en/media_center/press_release.asp?sCodigo=E-027/20, accessed October 5, 2020.

The Venezuelan government led by President Maduro rejected the plan. But it was not alone. Maduro's main opponent in the 2018 presidential election, Henri Falcón of the *Avanzada Progresista* ("Progressive Advance") party, also rejected the Pompeo-Guaidó plan and the deployment of U.S. warships off the Venezuelan coast. The removal of Maduro, he wrote, "is a process and not an imposition; it requires agreements between adversaries for it to be successful. The solution in Venezuela is between Venezuelans."[75] "The pandemic," he wrote, "is wreaking havoc in the world. Venezuela is one of the most vulnerable. It would be humanitarian and very great if ships came with aid and medicine, and it would be very inhumane if they came loaded with weapons and threats."[76]

Most of the opposition in Venezuela, like Falcón, did not approve of Guaidó's submission to Trump and Pompeo. Claudio Fermín of the *Partido Soluciones para Venezuela* ("Solutions for Venezuela Party") attacked the "irresponsible and fanciful thesis" of Guaidó and his supporters, which is reliant upon the "fantasy cloud of instructions sent to them by their bosses Elliott Abrams, Pompeo, and Trump."[77] Henrique Capriles Radonski, who twice ran unsuccessfully to be president, said that Maduro has "internal control" while

---

75 Henri Falcón, Twitter post, April 1, 2020, https://twitter.com/HenriFalconLara/status/1245093356629372936?s=20, accessed October 5, 2020.

76 Henri Falcón, Twitter post, April 2, 2020, https://twitter.com/HenriFalconLara/status/1245742474099859456, accessed October 5, 2020.

77 Claudio Fermín, "Ya no saben qué hacer," *El Tubazo Digital*, March 31, 2020, https://www.eltubazodigital.com/columnistas/claudio-fermin-ya-no-saben-que-hacer/2020/03/31/, accessed October 5, 2020.

Guaidó's people have "international alliances."[78]

So much of this is déjà vu. On October 7, 1963, U.S. President John F. Kennedy gathered his advisors in the White House to discuss how to overthrow the democratically elected government of João Goulart in Brazil. Kennedy asked frankly, "Do you see a situation coming where we might be—find it desirable to intervene militarily ourselves?" His ambassador in Brazil, Lincoln Gordon, said that he had worked on a plan with U.S. Southern Command—then based in Panama—and with his contacts in the Brazilian military. A U.S. invasion, Gordon told Kennedy, would require a "massive military operation," which "all depends on what the Brazilian military do." Any coup without major military support would lead to "the beginnings of what would amount to a civil war."[79]

Rather than risk a civil war, Gordon said the military had to act, and the United States had to provide them with diplomatic and military support. By March 1964, Gordon said that the "most significant development is the crystallizing of a military resistance group under the leadership of General Humberto Castelo Branco."[80] Washington gave the green light.

78 "Maduro convoca nuevo diálogo con la oposición para 'hablar sobre el coronavirus,'" *TalCual*, March 25, 2020, https://talcualdigital.com/maduro-convoca-nuevo-dialogo-con-la-oposicion-para-hablar-sobre-el-coronavirus/, accessed October 5, 2020.

79 Excerpts from John F. Kennedy's conversation regarding Brazil with U.S. Ambassador to Brazil Lincoln Gordon on Monday, October 7, 1963, Tape 114/A50, President's Office Files, John F. Kennedy Presidential Library, Boston, https://nsarchive2.gwu.edu/NSAEBB/NSAEBB465/docs/Document%209%20brazil-jfk%20tapes-100763-revised.pdf, accessed October 5, 2020.

80 "Telegram From the Ambassador to Brazil (Gordon) to the Department of State," *Foreign Relations of the United States, 1964–1968*, Volume XXXI, South and Central America; Mexico, Document 187, Office of the Historian, US State Department,

Operation Brother Sam was put in motion, which included egging on the Generals and sending a massive naval task force to sit off the coast of southern Brazil. An aircraft carrier, two guided missile destroyers, and other support vessels left Aruba and made their very public journey to Brazil. General Castelo Branco moved against Goulart; that coup created a military dictatorship—backed by Washington—that lasted 21 years and killed, detained, and tortured tens of thousands of people.

The U.S. carrier group that sits off the coast of Venezuela seems to be mimicking Operation Brother Sam of 1964. Rather than focus attention on the pressing problem of controlling the coronavirus in the United States—or even amongst its military forces—Trump has begun manoeuvres that could very well lead to a serious and dangerous clash in the Caribbean Sea.

THE COLOMBIAN PEOPLE REJECT THE HYBRID WAR AGAINST VENEZUELA

On November 21, 2019, the Colombian people took to the streets in massive numbers to reject the policies of the government led by President Iván Duque. In particular, the people voiced two main demands.[81] First, they wanted Duque's right-wing government to advance the 2016 Peace Accords between the government and the left-wing FARC (Revolutionary Armed Forces of Colombia). These Accords,

https://history.state.gov/historicaldocuments/frus1964-68v31/d187, accessed October 5, 2020.

[81] Zoe PC, "Nine reasons why Colombians are going on strike," *Peoples Dispatch*, November 21, 2019, https://peoplesdispatch.org/2019/11/21/nine-reasons-why-colombians-are-going-on-strike/, accessed October 5, 2020.

negotiated in good faith, would have ended a war that has lasted for six decades (70 percent of Colombian society has been born during this war). Second, the people wanted to end the harsh austerity policies driven by Duque's government, which includes cuts to public universities, the pension system, and broad social spending. The main trade union federation, the Central Trade Union of Workers in Colombia (CUT), called for that protest, which then broadened into a mass uprising against Duque and the system of Colombian politics.

The general secretary of the CUT and spokesperson of the People's Congress (*Congreso de los Pueblos*), Edgar Mojica, was on the barricades daily helping shape the mass upsurge that suggested that Colombian society no longer wanted to be held hostage to the whims of its sclerotic oligarchy and to the United States government. This was the mood. It was clear in the slogans and graffiti that emerged in Bogotá, the capital of Colombia, and then outwards to its smaller cities and towns. The two demands—to implement the Peace Accords and to end austerity—are related. The Colombian oligarchy fears that if it contributes to building a comprehensive and genuine peace, the arrival of the FARC onto the political stage will strengthen the left, and a stronger left will have the power to annul not only the austerity agenda but also the pro-U.S. orientation of the ruling classes of Colombia (for more on this, see the Tricontinental: Institute for Social Research dossier no. 23, *Peace, Neoliberalism, and Political Shifts in Colombia*[82]).

[82] "Peace, Neoliberalism, and Political Shifts in Colombia," Tricontinental: Institute for Social Research, dossier no. 23, December 3, 2019, https://www.thetricontinental.org/peace-neoliberalism-and-political-shifts-in-colombia/, accessed October

The other left organization—the National Liberation Army (ELN)—has in good faith tried to negotiate with Duque's government, but has seen the door slammed in its face repeatedly, as Pablo Beltrán, an ELN leader, told Argentine journalist and educator Claudia Korol last year. Duque has intensified the military campaign against the ELN.[83] If the Peace Accords with the FARC and the talks with ELN deepen, it would undermine the power of the oligarchy and of Washington. As Olimpo Cárdenas of the People's Congress said two years ago, "There is a sector of the Colombian oligarchy that benefits from the war."[84]

There are days when it seems as if President Duque cannot make decisions without consulting the U.S. government and his mentor, Álvaro Uribe. The advice he gets is to burrow deeper into an alliance with the United States, even at the cost of public opinion in Colombia. It would be fitting to call Duque's policy toward the United States a "doormat policy"—a policy where he offers Colombia as the doormat for the United States to wipe its feet before it marches into neighboring Venezuela. When we spoke to Mojica recently, he said, "The Colombian government is a submissive government. It is inclined toward the decisions of the North American government."

5, 2020.

83 "Exclusive Interview with Pablo Beltrán, Chief Negotiator of Colombia's ELN," *Peoples Dispatch*, February 9, 2019, https://peoplesdispatch.org/2019/02/09/exclusive-interview-with-pablo-beltran-chief-negotiator-of-colombias-eln/, accessed October 5, 2020.

84 Zoe PC, "'There is a sector of the Colombian oligarchy that benefits from the war,'" *Peoples Dispatch*, July 30, 2018, https://peoplesdispatch.org/2018/07/30/there-is-a-sector-of-the-colombian-oligarchy-that-benefits-from-the-war/, accessed October 5, 2020.

This is not a new development. At the start of the 20th century, Colombia's foreign policy was defined by the principle of *Respicium Polum* ("Look toward the North"). More recently, in the 1990s, U.S. foreign policy shifted its gaze from Central America to Colombia; Plan Colombia, developed in 1999, drove a militarized agenda of the U.S. and the Colombian oligarchy in the "War on Drugs," which was in essence a bid to defeat any revolutionary insurgency and consolidate control over the Andean-Amazon territory. What is indeed new, Mojica says, is that Duque has done everything to facilitate both the blockade against Venezuela and the potential military intervention into Venezuela.

When the governments of Canada and the United States urged their partners in Latin America to create a platform against Venezuela, which became the Lima Group in 2017, Colombia was an eager participant. In February 2019, Duque welcomed the Lima Group to Bogotá during a high-stakes gamble by the United States to overthrow the Venezuelan government of President Maduro. At that time, Mojica and other social movement leaders criticized the way their country was being used by the Colombian oligarchy and the United States for narrow purposes, against the interest of the Colombian people. Mojica told us, "We have been denouncing this for the past year, beginning when President Duque lent himself to legitimize Guaidó and to legitimize the positions that the Lima Group has had with respect to Venezuela." Heightened military tension with Venezuela suits the Duque government's agenda. It means that it can put off any talk of full implementation of the Peace Accords and cast aside any criticism of its austerity policies. Since 2016, hundreds of social movement leaders have been assassinated[85] across

[85] "Worldwide Protests Called Against Murder of Colombian Social

Colombia; this violence is obscured by the attention being paid by the media to the Colombian-Venezuelan border.

With the U.S. government absurdly saying that Venezuela is the source of narco-trafficking—even though all evidence pointing to narco-trafficking is rooted in Colombia—the pressure on Colombia to deal with its drug problem is now lifted. Indeed, the intimate links between the oligarchy and the narco-traffickers are now hidden by the hallucinatory claim that Maduro is himself involved in this trade.

Mojica told us that the entire narco-policy is a "distraction" because it fails to grasp the real problem. "We reject the policies of crop dusting and the blackmailing of the Colombian government" by the U.S., he said, which uses its international power to force policy changes on the country. Mojica explained that, because the production of coca leaves by small farmers is the "first step of production," and because the farmers have no other source of revenue to support their families, the farmers serve as "the weakest link in the chain" and an easy target for cocaine eradication programs.

These small farmers, whose farms and bodies will be saturated by toxic chemicals, are not the main culprits behind the drug trade, nor is their wellbeing the main concern of Duque's government; but they do provide a convenient scapegoat to mask the actions of those who really pull the strings. The responsibility for the colossal drug trade about which the Trump administration and his cronies are allegedly so concerned instead lies mainly with the large Colombian narco-cartels, who traffic the drugs through Mexico and Central America to North America; the drug mafia in North

Leaders," *Telesur*, July 22, 2019, https://www.telesurenglish.net/news/Worldwide-Protests-Called-Against-Murder-of-Colombian-Social-Leaders-20190722-0010.html, accessed October 5, 2020.

America itself; and the immense demand—largely in the U.S. and Europe—by consumers for South American cocaine.

But none of the main culprits face the brunt of the drug eradication policy, reserved instead for the "weakest link"—coca growers. "The coca growers and their families," Mojica said, "are not presented with any alternative in terms of financial support for the eradication of their crops." Despite this, they have unfairly become the frontline of the war. The 2016 Havana Peace Accords did provide a mechanism to assist farmers in transitioning from the cultivation of illicit crops. However, as with much else in the peace process, the protocol has not been respected; peasant communities have repeatedly denounced incidents of forced eradication by the army.[86] The assassination of the leaders of these communities is often carried out by paramilitary groups, cartels, and a section of the armed forces known as the *Fuerza Pública* ("Public Force").

The U.S. and the Duque administrations, Mojica says, are using the question of drugs to move an agenda for regime change in Venezuela. Matters are so grave that the Colombian government has allowed U.S. troops to enter its territory—both on the Caribbean coast and on the Venezuelan-Colombian border, such as in the area of Catatumbo. "We think that from there they are preparing a land invasion," says Mojica. These are tense times, with the imminent possibility of military manoeuvres turning into a war.

The Colombian Senate has been vocal in its opposition to the use of Colombian territory to destabilize Venezuela. In April 2020, a group of Colombian congressmen wrote

[86] Coccam Colombia, Twitter post, March 25, 2020, https://twitter.com/COCCAMColombia/status/1242601209174855682?s=20, accessed October 5, 2020.

a public letter to Duque saying that their country must not participate in regime change in Venezuela. If Duque wants to pursue any such agenda, he must seek permission from Congress. Mojica told us that the Colombian social movements "completely reject" Trump's agenda. "We are not its backyard," he said of the United States, and therefore not its doormat either. "We do not condone its anti-drug policies; we do not condone its policies of looting our natural resources and our environment."

THE BAY OF PIGLETS

In the early morning hours of Sunday, May 3, speedboats left the Colombian coastlines and headed toward Venezuela—though they had no authorization to cross the maritime border—and landed on the Venezuelan coastline at La Guaira.[87] This was clearly a hostile action, since the boats carried heavy weaponry, including assault rifles and ammunition. The people on the boats possessed satellite phones as well as uniforms and helmets with the flag of the United States of America. The incursion was intercepted by Venezuelan military (FANB), who fought them off; eight of the belligerents were killed, while two were intercepted, and several temporarily escaped. One of those who was arrested says that he is an agent of the U.S. government's Drug Enforcement Agency (DEA). Early Monday May 4, Venezuelan security forces, aided by the fishermen and

[87] "Venezuela arrests eight mercenaries part of 'Operation Gedeon,' including two US citizens," Peoples Dispatch, May 6, 2020, https://peoplesdispatch.org/2020/05/06/venezuela-arrests-eight-mercenaries-part-of-operation-gedeon-including-two-us-citizens/, accessed October 5, 2020.

fisherwomen of the Bolivarian Militias in the coastal town of Chuao, arrested eight additional mercenaries on a speed boat who were attempting to enter the country. Two others were captured by Venezuelan Security Forces the same day in the town of Puerto Maya. During the arrests, more weaponry and military intelligence equipment was seized by Venezuelan security forces.

Néstor Reverol, the minister of internal affairs of Venezuela, told Venezuelan television stations hours after the thwarted incursion that the government received information about the attack from sources in Colombia and from its own regular patrols of the Venezuelan coastline. "We cannot take any of their threats lightly," said senior Venezuelan politician Diosdado Cabello. "What happened today," he said, "is an example of the desperation" of the United States and its allies.

Such plots surround Venezuela, the plotters a cast of characters from the seediest quarters of the military and the drug world, as well as of U.S. intelligence and Colombian paramilitaries. The plot for a small invasion in 2019 that unraveled is now documented by Joshua Goodman of the Associated Press.[88] That plot was led by Jordan Goudreau, who served in the U.S. Army as a medic in Iraq and Afghanistan and then became a private security contractor; he worked with Cliver Alcalá, a former Venezuelan military officer, who brought together a few hundred Venezuelan military deserters to conduct the raid. Alcalá is now in prison in the United States for his involvement in the drug trade. Goudreau and Alcalá were backed by Trump's bodyguard

[88] Joshua Goodman, "Ex-Green Beret Led Failed Attempt to Oust Venezuela's Maduro," *Associated Press*, May 2, 2020, https://apnews.com/article/79346b4e428676424c0e5669c80fc310, accessed October 5, 2020.

Keith Schiller and Roen Kraft of Kraft Foods. The entire operation sniffs of a madcap CIA adventure, akin to the 1961 CIA failed invasion of Cuba at the Playa Girón.

One of the ugliest aspects[89] of the 2020 military incursion was that—in the name of combatting narco-trafficking—the entire operation seems to have been financed by drug dealers. José Alberto Socorro Hernández (alias Pepero), who was captured during the invasion, admitted that the La Guajira cartel of Colombia offered them $2 million for their actions. Pepero confessed that the operation was financed by Elkin Javier López Torres (alias *La Silla*, "The Chair," or *Doble Rueda*, "Double Wheel"), a relative of Alcalá's wife, Marta González.

It is likely that this most recent invasion in May 2020 emerged out of the military deserter camp set up by Alcalá in Colombia. One of the men involved in the raid was Captain Robert Levid Colina, also known as *Pantera* ("Panther"). Colina had been involved in the attempted coup on behalf of Juan Guaidó on April 30, 2019, and is a close associate of Alcalá's. Antonio Sequea, former Venezuelan National Guard member, who had last been seen[90] on April 30, 2019, during the failed *coup d'état* led by Leopoldo López and Juan Guaidó,[91] was among those arrested. Sequea is believed

89 Alexis Rodriguez, "Did he know or did he not know? Was Duque aware of a mercenary plan to kidnap Maduro?" video, https://www.elciudadano.com/en/did-he-know-or-did-he-not-know-was-duque-aware-of-a-mercenary-plan-to-kidnap-maduro/05/08/, accessed October 5, 2020.

90 Leopoldo López, Twitter post, April 30, 2019, https://twitter.com/leopoldolopez/status/1123169379661819904?s=20, accessed October 5, 2020.

91 "Guaidó is surprise guest at Trump's State of the Union," *Peoples Dispatch*, February 5, 2020, https://peoplesdispatch.org/2020/02/05/

to have led the operation. The arrest of two U.S. military officials from Texas, Luke Denman and Airan Berry, who are members of the U.S. mercenary company Silvercorp was also noteworthy. The U.S. government has denied all participation in the operation,[92] and has largely ignored it, but, according to one of the detained mercenaries, the pair has a relationship with Trump's head of security.

Silvercorp is the company of Jordan Goudreau, to whom Guaidó promised to pay $212.9 million to "capture, detain, or 'remove' President Nicolás Maduro and install him in his place," as reported by journalist Alan MacLeod.[93] In February 2019, Goudreau and his company provided security to the Venezuelan right-wing during the provocative Humanitarian Aid concert. Videos and photos have also emerged on social media showing a contract signed between Goudreau and right-wing opposition leader Guaidó.[94] The former U.S. special operative expressed frustration because Guaidó did not hold up his end of the bargain, however, and Silvercorp

guaido-is-surprise-guest-at-trumps-state-of-the-union/, accessed October 5, 2020.

92 "Pompeo: No US govt involvement in Venezuela overthrow plot," *Al Jazeera*, May 6, 2020, https://www.aljazeera.com/news/2020/05/06/pompeo-no-us-govt-involvement-in-venezuela-overthrow-plot/, accessed October 5, 2020.

93 Alan MacLeod, "Guaidó's mercenary hit contract on Venezuela's Maduro mirrors official US bounty, authorizes death squad killings," *The Grayzone*, May 10, 2020, https://thegrayzone.com/2020/05/10/guaido-mercenary-contract-venezuelas-maduro-us-bounty-death-squad/, accessed October 5, 2020.

94 "Read the attachments to the General Services Agreement between the Venezuelan opposition and Silvercorp," *The Washington Post*, May 7, 2020, https://www.washingtonpost.com/context/read-the-attachments-to-the-general-services-agreement-between-the-venezuelan-opposition-and-silvercorp/e67f401f-8730-4f66-af53-6a9549b88f94/, accessed October 5, 2020.

has yet to receive payment for their work.

The operation, which has been under investigation by Venezuelan authorities for the past couple of months, is believed to be organized, planned, and financed by the Venezuelan opposition and its diverse allies with the objective of assassinating constitutional president Nicolás Maduro and other high-level leaders of the Venezuelan government. It is likely that the U.S. government's bounty on Maduro and on other leaders played a role in this attempted invasion.

However, as Hernán Vargas, a member of the *Movimiento de Pobladoras y Pobladores* ("the Settlers' Movement") and the Secretary of ALBA Movements explained, it is likely that the mission of this group "was not to take over the country, it was not to take over the government. It was simply to carry out a series of activities that would be coordinated with other forces, which all depended on a chain of events that did not occur . . . They really expected maybe a response from the Armed Forces, a street mobilization, or that another armed group that was going to join, and that didn't happen."

The mercenaries playing freedom fighters, however, "did not expect the response of the people," Vargas said, and they vastly underestimated the skill of the Venezuelan intelligence. He explained that they likely had it in their heads that they could be "received with applause and with cheers. They thought people were going to support this or an Armed Force was going to support this . . . but there are no people in Venezuela willing to do that. The majority of Venezuelans want it to be resolved in peace. There are no sectors that are willing to take that gamble or not enough for what they need at this moment."

The threat, however, remains. Vargas calls for a close study of the Silvercorp contract with Juan Guaidó and Juan

José Rendón[95]—a right-wing political consultant and former advisor to Guaidó—where he states that there is, "a whole series of clauses that allow or agree to actions of human rights violations, the execution of civilians, or the use of heavy weapons, which introduce another dimension. In other words, this is an equally dangerous situation because these groups can easily carry out terrorist actions, and they also set strategic civilian and military objectives in Venezuela."

Vladimir Padrino López, the minister of defense of Venezuela, said that the government and the people had defeated this attack and would remain vigilant against other such plots. One of the characteristic features of the Bolivarian process has been the mobilization of the population to defend itself—from the attempted coup against Chávez in 2002 to today. "We declare ourselves in rebellion," Padrino said, adding that Venezuela is now under a state of "permanent vigilance." Despite the global pandemic, the old playbook of the CIA and the U.S. government as a whole—currently led by the Trump administration—with their dirty coups and hybrid wars, remains operational. Much like the Cubans who thwarted the attempted U.S.-backed invasion at the Playa Girón, or Bay of Pigs (1961), the Venezuelan people defeated this Bay of Piglets plot in La Guaira (2020).

95 Anthony Faiola, Karen DeYoung and Ana Vanessa Herrero, "From a Miami condo to the Venezuelan coast, how a plan to 'capture' Maduro went rogue," *The Washington Post*, May 7, 2020, https://www.washingtonpost.com/world/the_americas/from-a-miami-condo-to-the-venezuelan-coast-how-a-plan-to-capture-maduro-went-rogue/2020/05/06/046222bc-8e4a-11ea-9322-a29e75effc93_story.html, accessed October 5, 2020.

THE WEAKNESS OF U.S. POWER

Five Iranian tankers[96]—each laden with gasoline—moved swiftly with their flags flying and their radar open to detection from Bandar Abbas (Iran) into the Caribbean Sea. One of them, serendipitously named "Fortune," broke through the feverish U.S. naval blockade to enter El Palito, Venezuela, on May 24. That the U.S. was unable to force a confrontation with the Iranian vessels signals the weakness of the U.S. position. A new sea bridge opens between two countries under immense U.S. pressure; this demonstrates the limitations—but not the end—of U.S. power and of the hybrid war.

96 Vijay Prashad, "Why Iran's fuel tankers for Venezuela are sending shudders through Washington," *Peoples Dispatch*, May 26, 2020, https://peoplesdispatch.org/2020/05/26/why-irans-fuel-tankers-for-venezuela-are-sending-shudders-through-washington/, accessed October 5, 2020.

INTERVENTION OF AMBASSADOR SAMUEL MONCADA BEFORE THE SECURITY COUNCIL OF THE UNITED NATIONS

April 4, 2019

Mr. President,

Pence is misleading the United Nations. Yesterday the Organization of American States (OAS) did not accept the designation of a new representative of the Bolivarian Republic of Venezuela. What happened yesterday was that they accepted the designation of a representative of the National Assembly. Still, it is not clear what that person can do, as the OAS is an Organization of States, represented by the National Government, and not of National Assemblies. This legal absurdity took place as a result of the desires of Mr. Pence's government to carry out a *coup d'état* in the OAS and another in Venezuela. As such, we suggested that all parties become well informed over what was adopted yesterday in Washington. We warn that Mr. Pence's government will try the same trick here, within the General Assembly, and we trust that it will fail.

Mr. President,

The humanitarian situation in Venezuela needs to be resolved, but we will also err in the treatment if we err in the diagnosis. The situation, as has been affirmed here, is the result of human actions. But what has not been said is that these actions are part of a plan for economic destruction designed by the government of the United States and its ally, the United Kingdom, with the objective of strangling the national economy, causing maximum social suffering, eroding the capabilities of our nation to sustain itself and, ultimately, to spark an implosion that will allow for a foreign military intervention based on the nefarious notion of the responsibility to protect, which has been used as an excuse for colonial invasions of countries that have oil.

This is a gigantic, inhumane experiment of unconventional warfare. A policy of calculated cruelty that violates human rights on a massive scale, reaching the point of committing crimes against humanity, all with the goal of justifying pillaging and looting, imposing a local, subordinate government and, in our case, using a racist ideology that arose over 200 years ago, when the United States was a slave-owning nation, which today they promote in violation of international law. We refer to the infamous Monroe Doctrine. Listen to their own words.

On January 9, 2018, spokespersons from the State Department declared, "the pressure campaign is working . . . And what we are seeing . . . is a total economic collapse in Venezuela. So our policy is working, our strategy is working and we're going to keep it."

On October 12, 2018, Ambassador William Brownfield said: "We must treat this as an agony, a tragedy that will continue until it finally reaches an end . . . and if we can do something to accelerate it, we must do it, but we must do it understanding that this is going to have an impact on millions of people who are already having difficulties in finding food and medicines . . . We cannot do this and pretend that it will not have an impact, we have that to make a hard decision, the desired end justifies this severe punishment."

On March 7, 2019, Senator Marco Rubio stated that "Over the next few weeks, Venezuela is going to enter a period of suffering no nation in our hemisphere has confronted in modern history."

On March 22, 2019, John Bolton noted, "It's sort of like in Star Wars when Darth Vader constricts somebody's throat, that's what we are doing to the regime economically."

This is about deliberate economic destruction; it is the systematic application of aggression with the use of financial instruments, undue pressure, and the use of dominant market positions to influence the banking sector, private businesses and other nations that engage in legal trade with Venezuela, including even U.N. agencies. All with the goal of isolating the country from international trade and financing systems. If it were true that the Venezuelan government is killing its people, why would they need a massive wave of extortion to increase suffering? The interest in a social implosion is not ours; it is of those who wish to invade us.

It is a plan in which banks, insurance agencies and ships are used with a destructive power comparable to weapons of mass destruction. Without having those responsible face justice and without them suffering the moral sanctions they deserve. On January 30, 2019, John Bolton said, "My advice to bankers, brokers, traders, facilitators, and other businesses:

don't deal in gold, oil, or other Venezuelan commodities," while on March 29, 2019, Elliott Abrams said, "We impose our sanctions. What does the regime do? The regime tries to figure out other ways to get around them. It tries to find new customers. It tries to find new sources of imports. So, what do we do? We watch carefully, and we can see ships moving and we can see new contracts with new companies, and when we do, we talk to shippers or we talk to refiners or we talk to governments and we say you should not be doing that. That's what we're doing."

A repugnant aspect of this criminal policy of mass destruction is that it is accompanied by theft and pillaging, costing our nation over $137 billion. While they deprive our people of essential goods, provoking maximum suffering, they rob the Venezuelan people of over one hundred billion dollars. The profits from our refineries are used to pay debts to oil companies friendly to the Trump administration. Its friends with Venezuelan sovereign debt bonds receive special licenses to collect their profits from money stolen from our people. They announced a plan to put the country into debt by $70 billion and to use that money to pay for non-certified debts in suspicious financial dealings. We cannot forget that the Bank of England, which stole $1.2 billion in gold from our people using the excuses that they do not recognize President Nicolás Maduro and that they are complying with the Trump sanctions. The Bank of England is not an independent institution, as its government affirms; rather it acts as the enforcement arm of policies of conquest and pillage of the governments of Trump and Theresa May. It is the same colonial policy of the British Empire of over 200 years ago.

Mr. President,

This is the true cause of the Venezuelan situation; there is no other. Certainly, our people are suffering and our government, as the Secretary General can certify, is working intensely with the United Nations system to increase both the number of cooperation projects as well as the volume and capacities of those projects, particularly in the health, food, education, electricity and transportation sectors. The same is happening with regards to cooperation with the International Committee of the Red Cross, whose president met yesterday in Caracas with our Head of State to move forward in a direct mechanism that facilitates true neutral, impartial and independent aid. The same can be said of friendly countries who have provided assistance in peace and in respect for our sovereignty.

An element that cannot be underestimated by those who wage war on Venezuela is the strength of our national spirit, which grows in the midst of these difficulties. The macabre experiment of destruction is aiming to prove that economic crime does work, that peoples can be broken and will surrender in the face of an oppressive foreign power. However, they got it wrong in Venezuela. The induced collective suffering is being resisted with the growing organization of our people. Our National Bolivarian Armed Force has not fractured and is more united than ever. Our workers are reacting to the attacks against our vital infrastructure with a discipline that the aggressors had never seen. Yes, there is trouble, but it is not leading to a civil war. Today, our people are setting an example for the world on how to fight for peace.

It would be logical to think that the efforts of our government to overcome the difficulties caused by aggression would be recognized and supported by the international community interested in alleviating suffering. However, what we are witnessing is a new wave of economic extortion that severs our country's financial flows abroad and impedes action by the United Nations' own agencies, which at this time have not found a way to receive our money and process the purchases required to meet the needs of our population. Do you know why? Because the Trump administration is waging a terror campaign against commercial and financial agents that touch Venezuelan money. What the United States has attempted to do so far is not humanitarian aid, but a covert operation without the consent of Venezuela, violating our territorial integrity, with a continuous threat of use of force, and openly inciting a military uprising and civil war. This is Mr. Abrams's specialty.

Mr. President,

This Security Council, according to the provisions of Articles 24, 34 and 39 of the Charter, has the responsibility to maintain international peace and security and to determine the existence of threats to peace or acts of aggression. As such, we request that it determine:

the legal basis on which the United States and United Kingdom apply a program of economic destruction on Venezuela, without the express authorization of this Council;

the legal authority to apply the so-called secondary sanctions on countries that legally trade with Venezuela;

the legal basis on which the United States threatens Venezuela with the use of force.

the legal authority on which the United States and United Kingdom can appropriate our riches, making profits through extortion with the mass violation of the human rights of our people;

the legal basis on which the United States can intervene in affairs that are essentially under the internal jurisdiction of Venezuela.

To conclude, the diagnosis for the current situation is the result of a campaign of aggression by the United States and United Kingdom. The treatment cannot be a new dose of aggressive interventionism with a humanitarian façade. The solution is not found in donations from those criminals who wish to portray themselves as saviors; it is not in channels of humanitarian aid designed to provoke armed conflicts; it is not in donor conferences that obscure the looting of our nation. The treatment is in returning the money stolen from Venezuela; in the end of the commercial and financial blockade of our people; in the end of the sabotage to our infrastructure through covert operations; in the end of threats of military intervention; and in the end of threats against Venezuelans who wish to engage in dialogue. We must stop Trump's war. This Security Council must fulfill its mission, guaranteeing Venezuela its right to peace.

Thank you.

RIGHT TO REPLY TO THE ADDRESS BY THE DELEGATION OF PERU TO THE UNITED NATIONS ON THE ISSUE OF VENEZUELAN REFUGEES AND MIGRANTS

Even when they are surprisingly ignored by reports referred to here in this session, including those drafted by U.N. agencies, the criminal, unilateral sanctions have also resulted in an irrefutable increase in the migratory flow of Venezuelans, although we differ on the number mentioned here, considering that there has been a lack of due rigorousness in the methods to acquire such information, nor has there been a timely and verifiable provision of migration data by receiving country.

We should note, fortunately, that Venezuela has not been a recent victim of either a natural catastrophe or an armed conflict. The migration that we see today in the region, which is encouraged by extremist statements and by a psychological war that instills terror regarding the certainty of the future in Venezuela with the goal of weakening the morale of our people, is of an economic kind and is the direct result of a plan for the programmatic destruction of our economy.

We cannot allow a human right like freedom of movement to be securitized or politicized. On the country, this very Security Council would be engaging in a double standard in not promptly convening a session on the humanitarian and security crisis on the border, as declared by Trump on March 15, 2019.

THE VIOLENCE AND ECONOMIC DESTRUCTION CAUSED BY U.S. ECONOMIC SANCTIONS IN VENEZUELA

Joe Sammut and Gregory Wilpert

U.S. economic sanctions against Venezuela are a violent and illegal form of coercion, seeking regime change through collective punishment of the civilian population. The motives are fairly clear from the public statements of U.S. officials. The number of Venezuelans who have died as a result of these sanctions has been estimated in the tens of thousands, and this has certainly increased substantially over the past two and a half years that have elapsed since the last available mortality data.[97] These casualties may be even higher than would be expected to result from some military options that the Trump administration has said it is considering. Yet this state-sponsored violence receives very little attention in U.S. and international media. This chapter will look at the economic sanctions that the U.S. government has imposed

97 Mark Weisbrot and Jeffrey Sachs, *Economic Sanctions as Collective Punishment: The Case of Venezuela* (Washington, D.C.: Center for Economic and Policy Research, April, 2019).

on Venezuela. It will cover the damage that sanctions have done, including deaths and damage to human health, as well as economic damage. It will analyze the illegality of these sanctions, under both international and U.S. law. It will lastly discuss what can be done to eliminate the use of illegal economic sanctions and prevent them from killing more people and causing more suffering in Venezuela and other countries in the present, and future.

As this chapter is being finished, the Trump administration is continually tightening sanctions in ways that increase harm to civilians. For example, in June 2020 Copa Airlines was fined $450,000 for transporting passengers to Venezuela through Panama.[98] On the flight ban that was being enforced—which was not even officially part of what the U.S. government calls "economic sanctions"—the *New York Times* has reported that this decision "will be a heavy blow for millions of Venezuelans," because it will cut off access to remittances from relatives abroad. By banning airline courier services to Venezuela from Miami, the policy will make it much more difficult for many Venezuelans "to obtain scarce medication, spare parts and food."[99] The effect of this change alone was described as a "catastrophe for a lot of people" as it would "complicate enormously the transportation of humanitarian aid" by a spokesperson from Acción Solidaria,

[98] Reuters, "U.S. Fines Copa Airlines $450K for Transporting Passengers Between U.S., Venezuela," June 17, 2020, www.reuters.com/article/us-usa-copa-holdings-venezuela/u-s-fines-copa-airlines-450k-for-transporting-passengers-between-u-s-venezuelaidUSKBN23O3FTM, accessed July 1, 2020.

[99] Anatoly Kurmanaev, "U.S. Suspends Passenger and Cargo Flights to Venezuela," *New York Times*, May 15, 2019, www.nytimes.com/2019/05/15/world/americas/us-venezuela-flights.html, accessed July 1, 2020.

a medical NGO.

President Obama imposed sanctions against Venezuela with Executive Order 13692 in March of 2015. These sanctions targeted individuals in Venezuela, mostly officials of the Venezuelan government, and have generally been treated as though they caused no harm to the civilian population. However, these sanctions were a significant blow to an economy that was already hit very hard by falling oil prices. As *Reuters* noted at the time, "Declaring any country a threat to national security is the first step in starting a U.S. sanctions program."[100] Of course investors, lenders, buyers of Venezuelan oil, and everyone doing business with Venezuela knows what generally happens to countries that are declared a "national security threat" to the United States. By itself, this would make Venezuela's economic recovery more difficult, even before the more sweeping sanctions that were to come.

Declaring Venezuela "a national security threat" was not just harmful, dangerous, and obviously untrue, it was also a false declaration made in order to meet U.S. legal requirements for imposing these sanctions. This executive order, and the others imposing sanctions that followed, labeled Venezuela "an unusual and extraordinary threat to the national security" of the United States, which the law requires in order to impose sanctions. The executive order also stated

[100] Jeff Mason and Roberta Rampton, "U.S. Declares Venezuela a National Security Threat, Sanctions Top Offcials," *Reuters*, March 10, 2015, www.reuters.com/article/ us-usa-venezuela/u-s-declares-venezuela-a-national-security-threat-sanctions-top-offcials-idUSKBN0M51NS20150310, accessed July 1, 2020.

that Venezuela was creating a "national emergency" for the United States, a transparent legal fiction, required for the invocation of the 1976 National Emergencies Act.

The 2015 sanctions did some damage by reducing Venezuela's access to credit. For example, Citibank closed the accounts of Venezuela's Central Bank and the Bank of Venezuela in 2016 after conducting a "risk management review."[101] The 2015 sanctions also harmed the Venezuela economy by making it more difficult, or impossible, for high officials of the government to simply carry out official state business. In a country dependent on its state-owned oil industry for almost all of its foreign exchange earnings, this caused significant problems. There were no economic or statistical studies of the impact of the 2015 economic sanctions, so it is difficult to quantify how much damage they did.

The first sanctions to receive serious economic study were those imposed in August of 2017. Their impact was first evaluated by Francisco Rodríguez, a Venezuelan economist who is a leading expert on Venezuela's economy.[102] Rodríguez was the chief economic advisor to opposition presidential candidate Henri Falcón in the 2018 election. He has done extensive research on Venezuela, including developing some of most reliable estimations of economic statistics available after 2015, when the authorities stopped regular publication

[101] EFE, "Citibank Cites 'Risk Review' in Closing Some Venezuelan Accounts in U.S.," July 12, 2016, www.efe.com/efe/english/business/citibank-cites-risk-review-in-closingsome-venezuelan-accounts-u-s/50000265-2983786, accessed July 1, 2020.

[102] Francisco Rodríguez, "Crude Realities: Understanding Venezuela's Economic Collapse," September 20, 2018, https://venezuelablog.org/crude-realities-understandingvenezuelas-economic-collapse/, accessed July 1, 2020.

of many indicators. The 2017 sanctions were targeted at the financial sector, cutting off Venezuela from most borrowing in the United States and preventing a badly needed debt restructuring. International trade is reliant on short-term credit, and although there was an exception that prevented the 2017 sanctions from amounting to an effective trade embargo, the exception was overly limiting because an important part of trade credit for Venezuelan government entities exceeds the thresholds put in place by the executive order.[103] The result was the drying up of credit for trade and, especially, the credit-thirsty oil industry.

The financial toxification of Venezuela accelerated with the executive order. A September Financial Crimes Enforcement Network (FinCen) letter toxified business with Venezuela, the letter warning that "all Venezuelan government agencies and bodies, including SOEs [state-owned enterprises] appear vulnerable to public corruption and money laundering."[104] As a result, banks and other financial institutions closed Venezuelan accounts and tried to reduce their exposure to transactions from the country.[105] This had an extraterritorial effect: 95 percent of international dollar payments are made via the Clearing House Interbank Payments System (CHIPS), which is reliant on less than 50 correspondent banks that must have a branch office in the United States, leaving the system subject to U.S. law.[106]

103 Francisco Rodríguez (Coordinator), Guillermo Guerrero, and Adolfo De Lima, "A Humanitarian Oil Agreement for Venezuela," *Oil for Venezuela*, October, 2019, 32.

104 Rodríguez, "Crude Realities."

105 Ibid.

106 Daniel McDowell, "Financial Sanctions and Political Risk in the International Currency System," *Review of International Political Economy*, 2020, 7.

Without access to these correspondent banks, it is much more difficult and costly to make international transactions in dollars. This results in another negative knock-on effect on imports and other cross-border trades.

The massive loss of oil production caused severe economic damage to an economy that is dependent on oil exports for more than 90 percent of the dollars that it needs for imports. Venezuela has been, for many decades, a highly import-dependent economy. Thus, when imports fall drastically, so does overall output (GDP) and employment, and poverty increases dramatically. When the August 2017 sanctions hit, Venezuela had already been in recession for more than three years and had lost about a quarter of its GDP. As Mark Weisbrot and Jeffrey Sachs note, inflation was running at between 758 and 1,350 percent annually.[107] The country was already facing balance of payments problems, and difficulties meeting its foreign debt payments, all of which had already been exacerbated by the sanctions that began in March 2015, as well as a sharp fall in oil prices. Despite this, there was still a possibility of debt restructuring, in particular for the debt of PdVSA, the national oil company, which had $30 billion of debt. There were joint ventures that could borrow because they had oil revenue that was a form of collateral, and oil in the ground can also be securitized or even sold.

Indeed, it would seem odd that a country with the largest oil reserves in the world could go broke after oil prices had started to rise again. The sanctions blocked all of this, effectively ending the foundations of any economic recovery. The sanctions thus locked the country into a path of hyperinflation, debt default, and depression that continues to this day. This is worth emphasizing, since

[107] Weisbrot and Sachs, *Economic Sanctions as Collective Punishment*, 19.

economic recessions/depressions do not last indefinitely, and neither does hyperinflation. In fact, the median episode of hyperinflation since the Second World War in Latin America lasted just four months.[108] To get rid of hyperinflation, it is necessary to change people's expectations of what their money will be worth in the near future. Otherwise, its vanishing purchasing power becomes a self-fulfilling prophecy. Most hyperinflation is brought to an end by creating a new exchange rate system—known as an Exchange Rate Based Stabilization. In Bolivia in 1985, for example, this got rid of hyperinflation in ten days.[109] To escape from hyperinflation in this way, Venezuela's government would need access to a sufficient amount of dollars, and to the international financial system. The August 2017 financial sanctions took both of these away from Venezuela. This helped push Venezuela into hyperinflation and keep it there for most of the next three years.[110]

This continued loss of imports also deepened the depression in Venezuela's economy. Venezuela lost 745,000 barrels of its oil production, or about 36 percent, in the year following the beginning of those sanctions, as production fell from 1,942 to 1,239 barrels per day.[111] Today, it is just 570 barrels per day, down by 71 percent from before these sanctions.[112] The U.S. government added PdVSA to the list

---

108 Ibid, 20.

109 Jeffrey Sachs, "The Bolivian Hyperinflation and Stabilization," *The American Economic Review* 77, no. 2 (1987), 279–83.

110 Hyperinflation is generally defined by economists as inflation of at least 50 percent per month, or 13,000 percent at an annual rate.

111 Calculated from the October 2017 and October 2018 OPEC Monthly Oil Market Reports, www.opec.org/opec_web/en/publications/338.htm, accessed July 1, 2020.

112 December 2018 to May 2020. Calculated from March 2019 and June

of sanctioned entities in January 2019. These oil sanctions imposed by the Trump administration amounted to a trade embargo, cutting Venezuela off from its largest market (the United States received 35.6 percent of Venezuela's exports in 2018).[113] Even worse, the U.S. government used the threat of secondary sanctions against other countries to cut off other oil markets, as well as access to credit.[114] With this, as well as the effects of the 2017 FinCen letter and financial sanctions, the noose was tightened, cutting off Venezuela, not just from the United States, but also internationally.

One of the most devastating blows to the Venezuela economy was the recognition of the Juan Guaidó "government" of Venezuela, also in January 2019. In his new book, Bolton describes how important it was to the regime change effort:

> The more I thought about it, the more I realized the decision on political recognition was more important now than the oil sanctions. First, U.S. recognition would have major implications for the Federal Reserve Board, and therefore banks worldwide. The Fed would automatically turn control over Venezuelan government assets it possessed to the Guaidó-led Administration . . .

2020 OPEC Monthly Oil Market Reports, www.opec.org/opec_web/en/publications/338.htm, accessed July 1, 2020.

113 Weisbrot and Sachs, *Economic Sanctions as Collective Punishment*, 2.

114 See Francisco R. Rodríguez, "Sanctions and the Venezuelan Economy: What the
Data Say," *LatamEconomnics Viewpoint* (June 2019), https://franciscorodriguez.net/2020/01/11/sanctions-and-the-venezuelan-economy-what-the-data-say/; and Weisbrot and Sachs, *Economic Sanctions as Collective Punishment*, for further details of these impacts of the 2019 sanctions.

> the international financial consequences of recognition were nonetheless significant, since other central banks and private bankers weren't looking for reasons to be on the Fed's bad side. Second, the logic of sanctioning the country's oil monopoly, and other measures Mnuchin and Treasury were resisting, would become unanswerable once we endorsed Guaidó's legitimacy.[115]

Even worse, recognition of the Guaidó "government" would make Guaidó "the legal owner of funds or goods owned by the Venezuelan government." According to Weisbrot and Sachs, this meant the loss of "most of the government's $9 billion in reserves that [were] in gold; trade credits worth an estimated $3.4 billion; and CITGO, with estimated net assets of $5.2 billion."[116] The August 2017 sanctions also cut off some $2.5 billion annually of dividend payments from CITGO to the government.[117] By the same measure, any remaining access to correspondent banks was "mostly wiped out," which led to a situation where Venezuelans are denied the "necessary credits for importing medicine, food, and other essential goods."[118]

In August of 2019, President Trump's former National Security Adviser John Bolton upped the ante when he declared:

> one way to summarize this to a business for example, is do you want to "do business in Venezuela or do you want to

115 John Bolton, *The Room Where It Happened: A White House Memoir* (New York: Simon & Schuster, 2020), 253.

116 Weisbrot and Sachs, *Economic Sanctions as Collective Punishment*, 3.

117 Ibid., 7.

118 Ibid., 3.

do business with the United States?" And I think for any international corporations, whether they're U.S.-based, European, wherever they may be . . . they ought to be asking their management if it's worth risking for a trickle of income from the illegitimate Maduro government, if it's worth risking their business in the United States.[119]

He said this as his government issued Executive Order 13884, which froze all Venezuelan government assets in the United States and broadened the scope of secondary sanctions, leaving non-U.S. people and entities considered by the Treasury as having supplied "material assistance" liable to have their U.S. assets frozen. An advisory by a maritime legal firm highlighted that this could conceivably be used against ocean transportation services.[120] This fear was later realized, with shipping firms and tanker captains sanctioned.

As of May 2020, Venezuela produces just 570 barrels of oil per day, down 71 percent from what it produced before the August 2017 sanctions.[121] Furthermore, "to entice buyers wary of drawing scrutiny from the United States," reports *Reuters*, it is selling this oil at enormous discounts as

[119] Quoted in Teresa Bo, "US Sanctions on Venezuela Likely to Add to People's Woes," *Al Jazeera*, August 7, 2019, www.aljazeera.com/blogs/americas/2019/08/sanctions-venezuela-add-people-woes-190807080725031.html, accessed July 1, 2020.

[120] Freehill, Hogan & Mahar, "Client Alert: U.S. Increases Pressure on Venezuela with Issuance of Executive Order 13884," August 7, 2019, www.freehill.com/wp-content/uploads/2019/08/NYDOCS1-509645-v1-Client_Alert_on_Venezuela_-_Executive_Order_138841.pdf, accessed July 1, 2020.

[121] Calculated from October 2017 and June 2020 OPEC Monthly Oil Market Reports, www.opec.org/opec_web/en/publications/338.htm, accessed July 1, 2020.

compared to other countries.[122] In addition to the estimated 24.3 percent drop in GDP in the recession prior to the August 2017 sanctions, the economy shrank by an estimated 19.6 percent in 2018, and 25.5 percent in 2019.[123] This is the worst economic decline in Latin American history. In 2019, an estimated 32 percent of the population was "in crisis or worse" with regard to food needs.[124] *Bloomberg* reported that about one-fifth of Venezuela's food is being wasted, mostly because of fuel shortages.[125]

THE IMPACT OF SANCTIONS ON VENEZUELA'S POPULATION

It is well known that the kind of economic damage that Venezuela has seen under U.S. sanctions can kill people, and indeed it has. Weisbrot and Sachs looked at the increase in mortality between 2017 and 2018 and concluded that the 2017 sanctions had killed tens of thousands of people in a

122 Marianna Parraga and Luc Cohen, "Sanctions-Hit Venezuela Offers Big Discounts as Oil Prices Collapse: Traders," March 10, 2020, www.reuters.com/article/us-global-oil-venezuela/sanctions-hit-venezuela-offers-big-discounts-as-oil-prices-collapse-traders-idUSKBN20X33X, accessed July 1, 2020.

123 United Nations Economic Commission for Latin America and the Caribbean, "Preliminary Overview of the Economies of the Caribbean 2019–2020," June 2020, www.cepal.org/es/node/51648, accessed July 1, 2020.

124 Food Security Information Network, "2020 Global Report on Food Crises," 2020, https://docs.wfp.org/api/documents/WFP-0000114546/download/?_ga=2.171980321.347868695.1587462377-2130934537.1587462377, accessed July 1, 2020.

125 Nicolle Yapur, "A Fifth of Food Output is Wasted in Famine-threatened Venezuela," *Bloomberg*, June 26, 2020, www.bloomberg.com/news/articles/2020-06-25/a-fifth-of-food-output-is-wasted-in-famine-threatened-venezuela, accessed July 1, 2020.

year. This did not include the last four months of 2017. It is not difficult to see how the economic damage described above would lead to people dying. In their report, Weisbrot and Sachs provide some of the stark numbers: an 85 percent shortage of essential medicines; 80,000 HIV-positive people denied retrovirals since 2017; 16,000 needing dialysis; 16,000 with cancer; and 4 million with diabetes and hypertension who lack reliable access to insulin and cardiovascular medicine.[126]

Some 22 percent of children are stunted, according to data cited by the U.N., which also reported that "lack of access to water, soap, chlorine and other hygiene inhibits hand washing and household water treatment."[127] The deterioration in living standards is also clear from the massive increase in migration since 2015. The number of Venezuelans living abroad was almost 700,000 in 2015, a rise of 150,000 since 2010. By 2019, this number ballooned to 4,490,000.[128] For the six South American countries that the U.N. disaggregates by year, the number of Venezuelan arrivals registered in 2017 was 65,000; in 2018 it reached 240,000—an increase of 266 percent.[129] In 2019, the arrivals surpassed 860,000, another rise of 260 percent.[130]

The most recent data on mortality in Venezuela was

126 Weisbrot and Sachs, *Economic Sanctions as Collective Punishment*, 15.

127 United Nations, "Venezuela: Overview of Priority Humanitarian Needs," March 2019, 37, https://undocs.org/S/2019/345, accessed July 1, 2020.

128 United Nations, "Migration Trends in the Americas," 1, https://robuenosaires.iom.int/sites/default/files/Informes/Migration-Trends-in-the-Americas-October_o.pdf, accessed July 1, 2020.

129 Ibid., 2. The six South American countries are Argentina, Brazil, Ecuador, Paraguay, Peru, and Uruguay.

130 Ibid.

gathered by the National Survey on Living Conditions (ENCOVI), run by three universities in Venezuela. The group never released the data, but it found its way into the public view from a U.N. report that was distributed to major media. This data showed a 31 percent increase in mortality among the general population. Weisbrot and Sachs noted that this would mean an increase of more than 40,000 deaths, and concluded that tens of thousands of Venezuelans had died as a result of the 2017 sanctions.[131] Rodríguez estimates that in the year following the 2017 financial sanctions, Venezuela lost about $16.9 billion in oil revenue due to the decline in production.[132] This is an enormous amount of revenue with regard to the essential, and even life-saving imports—of medicine, medical equipment, and other imports—needed for public health. Total imports of medicine in 2018 were just U.S. $400 million, down 41 percent from 2017, and 88 percent below their level of $3.4 billion in 2012.[133] What would the government have done with an extra $16.9 billion of revenue? It is not difficult to imagine that they would have spent some of it on public health, including medicines, medical equipment, and the horribly deteriorated health, water, and sanitation infrastructure. It is also quite likely that many of the tens of thousands of doctors and medical professionals who left the country would have stayed in Venezuela.

We do not know all the reasons that various measures of public health and health indicators were deteriorating

131 Ibid.

132 Rodríguez, "Sanctions and the Venezuelan Economy, 35.

133 Instituto Nacional de Estadística, "Importaciones Capítulo," www.ine.gov.ve/index.php?option=com_content&view=category&id=48&Itemid=33, accessed July 1, 2020.

during the deep recession/depression that began in 2014. They were, however, clearly related to the collapse of the economy. It is also clear that the sharp drop of imports, the loss of credit, the loss of access to the international financial system, the balance of payments crisis, and most importantly the hyperinflation—which definitionally began after the 2017 sanctions—all contributed to the deep and prolonged depression. It is not difficult to imagine that in the absence of the powerful economic shock of the 2017 sanctions, the economy would have even begun to recover, the norm after more than three years of recession and especially for Venezuela, in the face of a sharp recovery in oil prices. In this case, mortality, which was elevated due to the collapse of the economy and public health, would have been expected to decrease. As a first approximation, it is not unreasonable to attribute the increase in mortality to the sanctions. Indeed, if there is ever a survey to measure mortality since the sanctions, it will probably show an accelerating annual increase from 2018 to 2020, even before COVID-19.

SANCTIONS AND COVID-19: TAKING ADVANTAGE OF THE CRISIS

The sanctions left Venezuela vastly more vulnerable to COVID-19. The shortages of vital medical supplies—in some cases, including shortages of soap and water—made it very difficult to follow the basic hygiene measures that reduce the spread of infection. A 2018 survey of hospitals conducted by an opposition political group and a medical NGO revealed the severe vulnerability of Venezuela's health system, with hospitals reporting problems, including non- or intermittently functioning laboratory testing, as well as shortages of water (79 percent), medicines (88 percent), and surgical supplies (79 percent).[134]

The world recession brought on by the pandemic had a drastic effect on oil prices, which fell further than they did in 2016, exacerbating the collapse of export earnings. In addition, remittances have been of growing importance to the Venezuelan economy, due to the massive outflow of migrants in the last few years. A May 2020 report by the *Inter-American Dialogue* estimated that 35 percent of Venezuelan households receive remittances.[135] The lockdown in foreign countries would affect this flow. Migrants tend to work in more precarious jobs and are thereby more exposed to the COVID-19-caused economic downturn, which has been severe even in the high-income countries.

Despite calls from members of the U.S. Congress, the U.N. High Commissioner for Human Rights, and the editorial board of the *Financial Times*, to ease sanctions as a response to the crisis, the U.S. government saw the crisis as an opportunity to increase the pressure on Venezuelans, in the hope of forcing the government from power.[136] As *NPR* put

---

134 Kathleen R. Page, Shannon Doocy, Feliciano Reyna et al., "Venezuela's Public Health Crisis: A Regional Emergency," *The Lancet* 393 no. 10177 (2019), 1254–60.

135 Manuel Orozco and Kathryn Klaas "Money Transfers to Venezuela: Remittance Flows Amidst Evolving Foreign Exchange," *Inter-American Dialogue*, May 15, 2020, 9, www.thedialogue.org/analysis/money-transfers-to-venezuela-remittance-flows-amidst-evolving-foreign-exchange/, accessed July 1, 2020.

136 Jack Detsch, "Democrats Push Back on Sanctions, Citing Coronavirus Fears," *Foreign Policy*, March 27, 2020, https://foreignpolicy.com/2020/03/27/democrats-coronavirus-sanctions-waivers-iran-venezuela/, accessed July 1, 2020; U.N. News, "Ease Sanctions Against Countries Fighting COVID-19: UN Human Rights Chief," March 24, 2020, https://news.un.org/en/story/2020/03/1060092,

it, the combination of the health crisis and crash of oil prices weakened the government and has prompted "the U.S. to intensify efforts to drive [Maduro] from power."[137] As Elliott Abrams described, the United States had decided to ramp up the pressure on all "critical points in [Venezuela's] petroleum sector from production to shipping to the customers."[138] The aggressive, extraterritorial enforcement of sanctions included the February sanctioning of a subsidiary of the Russian oil company Rosneft, causing it to cease trading Venezuelan oil and sell its Venezuelan assets.[139] This impacted the dwindling number of other purchasers of Venezuelan oil. Refiners in India stopped purchasing in March.[140] The United States also began to sanction the transport of Venezuelan oil, leveling individual sanctions on tanker captains and vessels,

accessed July 1, 2020; The Editorial Board, "This is the Time to Waive Sanctions on Venezuela," *Financial Times*, March 30, 2020, www.ft.com/content/d6d42564-703c-11ea-9bca-bf503995cd6f, accessed July 1, 2020.

137 Phillip Reeves, "Many Venezuelan Hospitals Lack Basics to Function, Let Alone Handle COVID-19," *NPR*, April 10, 2020, www.npr.org/2020/04/10/831569313/many-venezuelan-hospitals-lack-basics-to-function-let-alone-handle-covid-19, accessed July 1, 2020.

138 Humeyra Pamuk, "Trump Administration to Step Up Pressure Campaign on Venezuelan Oil—US Envoy," *Reuters*, February 24, 2020, www.reuters.com/article/us-usa-sanctions-venezuela/trump-administration-to-step-up-pressure-campaign-on-venezuelan-oil-us-envoy-idUSKCN20I26S, accessed July 1, 2020.

139 Gabrielle Tétrault-Farber and Olesya Astakhova, "Rosneft Sells Venezuelan Assets to Russia after U.S. Sanctions Ramp Up," *Reuters*, March 28, 2020, www.reuters.com/article/us-russia-rosneft-venezuela/rosneft-sells-venezuela-operations-to-russian-state-firm-idUSKBN21F0W2, accessed July 1, 2020.

140 Lucia Kassai, "Venezuela Oil Crisis Deepens with India Refiners Halting Imports," *Bloomberg*, June 26, 2020, www.bloomberg.com/news/articles/2020-06-25/venezuela-oil-crisis-deepens-with-india-refiners-halting-imports, accessed July 1, 2020.

leading a number of shipping firms to cease transporting Venezuelan oil.[141]

Worse, a number of the measures seem deliberately targeted at trades which have obvious and direct humanitarian consequences. An oil-for-food and humanitarian supplies deal between Venezuela and several Mexican companies was targeted in June, with the companies and their owners blacklisted, forcing the trade to end before receipt of the food.[142] According to legal experts on international compliance, the deal had been deliberately crafted to take advantage of the humanitarian exception to the sanctions.[143] These events show

141 Humeyra Pamuk and Matt Spetalnick, "U.S. Puts Sanctions on Five Iranian Ship Captains for Bringing Oil to Venezuela," *Reuters*, June 24, 2020, www.reuters. com/article/us-venezuela-iran-gasoline/u-s-sanctions-five-iranian-ship-captains-for-bringing-oil-to-venezuela-pompeo-idUSKBN23V25I, accessed July 1, 2020; Jonathan Saul, "Greek Ship Managers Halt Venezuela Trade as U.S. Sanctions Bite," *Reuters*, June 15, 2020, www.reuters.com/article/us-venezuela-usa-tankers/greek-ship-managers-halt-venezuela-trade-as-u-s-sanctions-bite-idUSKBN23M1TX, accessed July 1, 2020.

142 About 500 water trucks were delivered before the end of the trade, but according to the company, the sharp fall in the price of oil affected the delivery schedule of the planned corn delivery. Daphne Psaledakis and Marianna Parraga, "U.S. Slaps Sanctions on Mexican Firms, Individuals Linked to Venezuelan Oil Trade," *Reuters*, June 18, 2020, www.reuters.com/article/us-venezuela-politics-usa/u-s-slaps-sanctions-on-mexican-firms-individuals-linked-to-venezuelan-oil-trade-idUSKBN23P3D6, accessed July 1, 2020. The United States alleges that the prices charged were "grossly inflated," but even if that were the case, there is no dispute that some humanitarian supplies were delivered through the deal. US Treasury, "Press Release: Treasury Targets Sanctions Evasion Network Supporting Corrupt Venezuelan Actors," June 18, 2020, https://home.treasury.gov/news/press-releases/sm1038, accessed July 1, 2020.

143 Evan Abrams, Peter Jeydel, Brian Egan, and Ed Krauland, "Three Key Takeaways from OFAC's Latest Venezuela Sanctions Actions,"

the superficial nature of the U.S. government's humanitarian exception. As noted by Rodríguez, "it is reasonable to believe that the exception could have been used only if it was as a result of an underlying agreement between the government and the opposition," leaving the humanitarian needs of Venezuelans hostage to an unlikely deal with the Guaidó-led opposition, which has called for the immediate resignation of President Maduro as a precondition for negotiations.[144]

THE STRATEGY, AND ILLEGALITY, OF COLLECTIVE PUNISHMENT

U.S. Secretary of State Mike Pompeo has not tried to hide what the sanctions are doing or intended to do. On March 11, 2019 he had the following exchange with *Associated Press* Reporter Matt Lee:

> MATTHEW LEE: Are you satisfied with the pace of the momentum behind Guaidó and his leadership? . . .
>
> MIKE POMPEO: Well, we wish things could go faster, but I'm very confident that the tide is moving in the direction of the Venezuelan people and will continue to do so. It doesn't take much for you to see what's really going on there. The circle is tightening, the humanitarian

Steptoe International Compliance Blog, June 22, 2020, www.steptoeinternationalcomplianceblog.com/2020/06/three-key-takeaways-from-ofacs-latest-venezuela-sanctions-actions/#page=1, accessed July 1, 2020.

144 Rodríguez et al., "A Humanitarian Oil Agreement for Venezuela, 31; EFE, "Guaidó reitera que solo dialogará si se concreta salida de Maduro del poder," *Última Hora*, February 6, 2019, www.ultimahora.com/guaido-reitera-que-solo-dialogara-si-se-concreta-salida-maduro-del-poder-n2796277.html, accessed July 1, 2020.

crisis is increasing by the hour. I talked with our senior person on the ground there in Venezuela last night, at 7:00 or 8:00 last night. You can see the increasing pain and suffering that the Venezuelan people are suffering from.[145]

This is consistent with his, and the Trump administration's, use of sanctions against Iran. As noted by Human Rights Watch, Pompeo told CBS News on February 14, 2019: "Things are much worse for the Iranian people [with the U.S. sanctions], and we are convinced that will lead the Iranian people to rise up and change the behavior of the regime."[146] Senator Marco Rubio, considered to be a major influence on the Trump administration's Latin America policy, expressed satisfaction that "Maduro's days are numbered" because "he can't access funds to rebuild the electric grid and he can't end the sanctions."[147] This certainly looks like a strategy of collective punishment, and one that has killed civilians, for example with blackouts shutting down medical equipment in hospitals. The implication is that the government will be toppled because it cannot end the suffering caused by the sanctions. On February 8, 2019 a senior White House official told *Reuters* that the U.S. government was "holding direct communications with members of Venezuela's military urging them to abandon President Nicolás Maduro and is

145 Weisbrot and Sachs, *Economic Sanctions as Collective Punishment*, 17–18.

146 Human Rights Watch, "Iran: Sanctions Threatening Health," October 29, 2019, www.hrw.org/news/2019/10/29/iran-sanctions-threatening-health, accessed July 1, 2020.

147 Marco Rubio, Twitter post, May 16, 2019, https://twitter.com/marcorubio/status/1129115646007099392?lang=en, accessed July 1, 2020.

also preparing new sanctions aimed at increasing pressure on him."[148]

These sanctions violate U.S. law. They also violate international law, including treaties that the United States has signed. This can be seen clearly in Articles 19 and 20 of the Charter of the Organization of American States:

> Article 19: No State or group of States has the right to intervene, directly or indirectly, for any reason whatever, in the internal or external affairs of any other State. The foregoing principle prohibits not only armed force but also any other form of interference or attempted threat against the personality of the State or against its political, economic, and cultural elements.
>
> Article 20: No State may use or encourage the use of coercive measures of an economic or political character in order to force the sovereign will of another State and obtain from it advantages of any kind.

Clearly this regime change effort violates the OAS charter. It violates the U.N. Charter and international human rights law, according to legal experts.[149] It violates prohibitions on

[148] Luc Cohen, Matt Spetalnick, and Roberta Rampton, "Exclusive: U.S. in Direct Contact with Venezuelan Military," *Reuters*, February 8, 2019, www.reuters.com/article/us-venezuela-politics-military-exclusive/exclusive-us-in-direct-contact-with-venezuelan-military-urging-defections-source-idUSKCN1PX22L, accessed July 1, 2020.

[149] See Matthew Happold and Paul Eden, eds., *Economic Sanctions and International Law* (Oxford: Hart Publishing, 2016); and Ella Shagabutdinova and Jeffey Berejikian, "Depoloying Sanctions While Protecting Human Rights: Are Humanitarian 'Smart' Sanctions Effective?" *Journal of Human Rights* 6, no. 1 (2007), 59–74; Weisbrot and Sachs, *Economic Sanctions as Collective Punishment*.

collective punishment that form part of both the Geneva and Hague conventions, of which the United States is also a signatory.[150] These conventions and prohibitions apply legally only during war time but this is an historical coincidence. It does not make sense that something which is a war crime when committed while people are shooting and killing each other should not be a crime when done during peacetime.[151]

CONCLUSION

It is clear that the U.S. sanctions against Venezuela have caused considerable suffering and death and constitute a serious crime. Although they currently remain in effect, there is grassroots organizing against them in the United States, as well as other countries whose governments have joined Trump's "coalition of the willing" for regime change in Venezuela. It is beyond the scope of this chapter to describe the political forces involved in this struggle, but it is important to call attention to it, because the U.S. government will sooner or later lose the power to use structural and economic violence in order to choose the governments of other countries.

Within the United States, some of the most successful past efforts to rein in this type of aggression have targeted the U.S. Congress. This is beginning to bear some fruit. For example, Representative Ilhan Omar has introduced the

150 Weisbrot and Sachs, *Economic Sanctions as Collective Punishment*, 18–19.

151 Office of the High Commissioner for Human Rights, "Unilateral Sanctions Must be Dropped, Says UN Expert," U.N. Human Rights (October 17, 2018), www.ohchr.org/en/NewsEvents/Pages/DisplayNews.aspx? NewsID=23731&LangID=E, accessed July 1, 2020.

"Congressional Oversight of Sanctions Act," which would require Congressional approval for sanctions imposed by the president. This is similar to the 1973 War Powers Resolution, in that it would take away from the president some of their power to harm other countries. This is part of a culmination of pushback from Congress against U.S. regime-change efforts in Venezuela since 2014, including a number of letters and statements from progressive members of Congress. Although it's not yet close to moving the Democratic leadership, this was true a couple of years ago for the efforts to invoke the War Powers Resolution against U.S. military involvement in the genocidal war in Yemen. In the spring of 2019—as a result of the same type of grassroots organizing we are seeing in Venezuela—both Houses of Congress voted to order President Trump to remove the U.S. military from that war. Although Trump has so far refused to get out, it was a historic, unprecedented vote, and probably would have moved a more "normal" president to exit. There is a good chance that the next U.S. administration will be forced to abandon its efforts at regime change in Venezuela, as well as the war in Yemen.

Over the longer run, the U.S. government will not be able to get away with these types of crimes. This could never have happened even as recently as 2013, when independent, left governments were elected in countries containing the majority of Latin Americans. Currently, Washington has a number of right-wing allies in power. Most of these regimes came to power with help from their U.S. patron, including in Brazil, Ecuador, Honduras, and Bolivia, the latter two taking power in U.S.-backed military coups. Colombia, Peru, and Paraguay (also victim of a U.S.-supported coup) have also allied with Trump. This is not sustainable, and it will change in the next few years, as it has changed in the latest Mexican and Argentinian elections.

The world is also changing, and the United States will not forever be able to control and weaponize the international financial system as it does today, with more than 60 percent of central bank reserves, and most of commerce, in dollars. The Chinese economy is already bigger than that of the United States, and within a decade it will be more than twice as big, on a purchasing power parity basis—which economists use for international comparisons. Yet Venezuela and other countries suffering from U.S. aggression cannot wait for these world-historical shifts toward a more multi-polar world. The United States will also have to change from within.

HOW U.S. SANCTIONS ENABLE THE THEFT OF VENEZUELA'S MOST VALUABLE ASSET

Anya Parampil

As the U.S. public's support for traditional forms of war-making wanes, the U.S. government has turned to more sophisticated, but no less cruel methods of hybrid warfare to achieve its foreign policy goals. Rather than wage war with its military, the United States has weaponized the international financial system in its efforts to weaken governments which oppose its imperial interests. In the case of Venezuela, the United States has unleashed an unprecedented economic war designed not only to overthrow the country's elected government, but to shatter its socialist experiment.

Over a year since the United States recognized Juan Guaidó as the President of Venezuela, Washington has yet to change reality on the ground in the country. Nicolás Maduro, Venezuela's democratically elected president, remains firmly in charge of his government, military, and the nation as a whole. Meanwhile, Guaidó's attempt to rally supporters for a day of national protest on November 16, 2019 exposed dwindling interest in his failed movement. "This is the first time I see a protest like this," reported Ana

Herrero, a *New York Times* correspondent based in Caracas. "In all the classic opposition spots, there is no one to be seen."[152] Yet where U.S. policy failed politically, it succeeded economically. While Trump's recognition of Guaidó had zero effect on who controls the streets of Caracas, his coup attempt did successfully change who controls Venezuela's internationally stored wealth. By freezing Venezuela's U.S.-based assets, economic sanctions have effectively transferred that capital and property—with an estimated worth of at least $7 billion—into the hands of the U.S. Treasury. Most shockingly, U.S. economic warfare has placed Venezuela's most valuable international asset, CITGO Petroleum, on the verge of total liquidation.

U.S. sanctions policy enabled the outright theft of Venezuela's international wealth. Such naked piracy was only possible thanks to the U.S. historically unrivaled strength as an empire, demonstrated most clearly in its hegemonic control of the international financial system. To aid its theft at this scale, Washington relied on the compliance of several Venezuelan opposition figures based in the United States, while posing as ambitious politicians, are revealed as agents of the U.S. oil industry and international finance upon closer examination. The case of Venezuela illustrates the essence and evolution of U.S. imperialism by exposing its growing reliance on financial warfare as a weapon of regime change. The democratic, socialist state of Venezuela presents the perfect enemy for the U.S. empire at this stage in capitalism's

[152] Ana Vanessa Herrero (AnaVHerrero), "In #Caracas: this is the first time I see a protest like this. In all the classic opposition spots, there is no one to be seen," Twitter post, November 16, 2019, 10:17 a.m., https://twitter.com/AnaVHerrero/status/1195722633561722882?s=08, accessed December 29, 2019.

development.

The policy adhered to by administrations of both U.S. parties toward Venezuela since the country's Bolivarian Revolution in 1999 can be objectively described as imperialist. Here, it is essential to maintain an accurate understanding of this system's characteristics. The concept of imperialism was most clearly defined by Russian revolutionary Vladimir Lenin in his 1917 work, *Imperialism: The Highest Stage of Capitalism*. Lenin described imperialism as a stage of capitalism in which industry and capital have merged into monopolies controlled entirely by a financial oligarchy which seeks to expand beyond national borders in order to exploit markets and resources. In Lenin's eyes, the First World War was the apotheosis of imperialism, as the great European powers sacrificed millions of their own citizens in a competition for world domination.

A century later, the United States of America—a European settler- colonial project—stands alone as the world's premier capitalist empire. But "the end of history" proclaimed by neoliberal triumphalists after the fall of the Berlin Wall failed to arrive, not merely due to capitalism's inability to cease its enterprise of continuous expansion, but due to the fact that the socialist ideal had not expired alongside the U.S.S.R. At a time when the United States was checking regime change targets off its hit list in a series of ghastly wars, from Belgrade to Baghdad, a Venezuelan colonel, Hugo Chávez Frías, was leveraging the world's largest oil reserves into a project he would eventually describe as "21st century socialism." Chávez not only transformed Venezuela; his model became an engine for the so-called Pink Tide of progressive governments seeking economic independence and political integration across Latin America.

As the United States reoriented itself from the failed wars of the Middle East, it began to strike back at Venezuela's revolutionary project with the weapons of hybrid warfare. Without tanks rolling on Caracas, without infantrymen sent recklessly into grinding urban warfare that risked returning them to their families without their limbs, or their lives—and therefore, without risking massive public protests and political rancor back home, the United States instead relied on its foundation as an empire: its monopolistic control of the international financial system. The key weapon in its arsenal against Venezuela's socialist project—its nuclear bomb—was financial sanctions.

Today, Venezuela faces the equivalent of a medieval starvation siege. The Washington, D.C.-based Center for Economic and Policy Research (CEPR) found that between 2016 and 2018, Venezuela experienced no less than 40,000 excess deaths as a direct result of U.S. sanctions. The U.S. State Department published what amounted to a list of sadistic confessions, boasting of its ability to devastate Venezuela's oil industry and prevent it from participating in the international market. (The dastardly document was inexplicably deleted within 24 hours of its publication.) The United States may have failed in its bid to determine who rules in Caracas. However, it has managed to transfer Venezuelan state bank accounts to the control of an unelected opposition, and Western financial institutions.

Since the United States launched its coup attempt in Venezuela, I have spent two months on the ground in Caracas covering the situation as it unfolded in the streets, as well as in conference halls where diplomats from across the world gathered for the ministerial meeting of the Non-Aligned Movement. While outside the country, I have dedicated my reporting to exposing the machinations of the exiled Venezuelan opposition as they acted as agents of a plot to loot Venezuela's internationally stored wealth. Through my coverage, I learned that Guaidó's U.S.-based minions were enabling the liquidation of CITGO, Venezuela's most valuable foreign asset. Through the scandal that I uncovered, I was able to illustrate in clear terms how the United States wields the emerging modalities of hybrid warfare to expand its control of global markets and resources.

"FINANCIAL TERRORISM" AND THE CITGO SCANDAL

Today, 21 countries are listed as sanctioned on the Treasury Department's Office of Foreign Asset Control website.[153] During the 2019 Ministerial Meeting of the Non-Aligned Movement (NAM), Russia's Deputy Foreign Minister, Sergey Ryabkov, said that according to his government's internal analysis, approximately 30 percent of the world's population lives under some form of U.S. economic sanctions.[154] During that summit, which took place in Caracas as Venezuela's three-year-long NAM chairmanship wound to an end, foreign ministers and other high-ranking diplomats from around the world united in opposition to Washington's intensifying global economic war. One by one, officials from Venezuela, Nicaragua, Cuba, Zimbabwe, Iran, Syria,

[153] US Department of the Treasury, "Sanctions Programs and Country Information," www.treasury.gov/resource-center/sanctions/Programs/Pages/Programs.aspx, accessed December 29, 2019.

[154] Anya Parampil, "World 'Will Diminish Role of Dollar and US Banking System': Russian Minister at Non-Aligned Movement," *Grayzone*, July 26, 2019, video, 18:24, www.newcoldwar.org/world-will-diminish-role-of-dollar-and-us-banking-system-russian-minister-at-non-aligned-movement/, accessed December 29, 2019.

North Korea, and beyond took to the floor to decry the suffering U.S. policy had inflicted on their populations. During his address, Iranian Foreign Minister Javad Zarif urged his colleagues to cease using the familiar term "sanctions." According to Zarif, Washington was not merely "sanctioning" its enemies, but waging "economic terrorism" against them. "Just Google 'terrorism,'" Zarif advised his counterparts, waving his mobile phone up in the air. "This is the definition that the dictionary will give you: 'unlawful use of violence or intimidation, especially against civilians, in pursuit of political gains' . . . please friends, stop using [the term] 'sanctions!'" he thundered. "Sanctions have a legal connotation. This is economic terrorism . . . we have to say it again and again!"[155]

For Venezuela, "economic terrorism" has manifested as a series of measures designed not merely to cut off its access to the international market, but to transfer billions of dollars' worth of the country's international assets into the hands of foreign capitalists. For example, when U.S.-imposed financial restrictions prevented Caracas from paying back a loan issued by Citibank, the financial institution opted to liquidate approximately $1.4 billion worth of Venezuelan gold reserves stored in its vaults.[156] Similarly, in an act of expropriation,

---

155 Anya Parampil, "'We are the Vaccine Against Unilateralism': Non-Aligned Movement Gathers in Venezuela to Resist Dictatorship of Dollar," *Grayzone*, July 28, 2019, https://thegrayzone.com/2019/07/28/we-are-the-vaccine-against-unilateralism-the-non-aligned-movement-gathers-in-venezuela-to-resist-the-dictatorship-of-the-dollar/, accessed December 29, 2019.

156 Mayela Armas and Corina Pons, "Citigroup to Sell Venezuelan Gold in Setback to President Maduro: Sources," *Reuters*, March 20, 2019, www.reuters.com/article/us-venezuela-politics-gold/citigroup-to-sell-venezuelan-gold-in-setback-to-president-maduro-sources-

the Bank of England has refused to repatriate $1.2 billion worth of Venezuelan gold since January 2019.[157] Yet perhaps the greatest testament to the economic war against Caracas has come in the form of U.S. attempts to liquidate CITGO, Venezuela's most valuable international asset.

In the summer of 2019, a U.S. court ruled that a Canadian gold mining firm called Crystallex International had the right to seize $1.4 billion worth of the oil refinery's shares as compensation for money owed by the Venezuelan government. The court's decision was made possible thanks to several steps taken by the U.S.-recognized Venezuelan coup regime, and its "Attorney General," a corporate lawyer named José Ignacio Hernández. Following the Trump administration's recognition of Guaidó in January 2019, Hernández assumed the role of Venezuela's top legal representative in the United States. Hernández then proceeded to allow Venezuela's legally defunct, opposition-led National Assembly to directly appoint the corporate board of CITGO Holding and CITGO Petroleum, two private, U.S.-based corporations. Prior to the Guaidó takeover, the Venezuelan government was the only body allowed to select the board of Petroleos de Venezuela (PdVSA), Venezuela's state-owned oil company. PdVSA's board then appointed a board to PdVSA Holding, which appointed the board of CITGO Holding, which appointed the board of CITGO Petroleum. Under Hernández's watch, the separation between CITGO, a PdVSA subsidiary and private corporation, and the Venezuelan state was completely

idUSKCN1R12GR, accessed December 29, 2019.

157 Patricia Laya, Ethan Bronner, and Tim Ross, "Maduro Stymied in Bid to Pull $1.2 Billion of Gold from U.K.," *Bloomberg*, January 25, 2019, www.bloomberg.com/news/articles/2019-01-25/u-k-said-to-deny-maduro-s-bid-to-pull-1-2-billion-of-gold, accessed December 29, 2019.

upended.

As luck would have it, Crystallex's entire legal claim against CITGO was based on the idea that the oil refinery was not a private corporation, but rather an "alter ego" of the Venezuelan state. Shortly after Guaidó's shadow government directly appointed CITGO management, Crystallex filed a court motion charging his regime with "complete disregard for corporate formalities" over its direct appointment of the CITGO boards. According to Crystallex, the move was "hardly a sign of [CITGO Holding and CITGO Petroleum's] independence from government control."[158] The U.S. court agreed, ruling in Crystallex's favor on July 29.[159] Within a matter of months, the actions of Guaidó's U.S.-recognized administration had managed to aid a foreign corporation's legal fight to seize part of Venezuela's most prized asset. How was such incompetence possible? Members of Venezuela's moderate opposition who were outraged by the possible theft of their country's most valuable foreign asset turned to me to explain why Crystallex's victory was no mistake. Chief among them was financial analyst Jorge Alejandro Rodríguez, who told me shortly after the court's decision that it was not incompetence, but rather "a fraud [perpetrated] against [Venezuela's] National Assembly" that had led to the

158 *Crystallex International Corp. vs. Bolivarian Republic of Venezuela*, nos. 18-2797, 18-3124 (3d Cir. 2019), www.scribd.com/document/405833173/Crystallex-International-Corp-v-Bolivarian-Republic-of-Venezue-03cae-18-02797-13208533-0, accessed December 29, 2019.

159 "Court Ruling Against Venezuela in Crystallex Case Puts Citgo at Risk," *Reuters*, July 29, 2019, www.reuters.com/article/us-venezuela-pdvsa-crystallex/court-ruling-against-venezuela-in-crystallex-case-puts-citgo-at-risk-idUSKCN1UO1L6, accessed December 29, 2019.

fateful ruling.[160] At the center of the scheme was Guaidó's "Attorney General," José Ingacio Hernández.

In a series of conversations, Rodríguez—a fervent opponent of Venezuelan President Nicolás Maduro—revealed to me that he had met with Venezuelan lawmakers in June in order to warn them that CITGO was on the verge of liquidation. He told them how their direct selection of CITGO's board had helped legal cases lodged against the company in the United States while chastising Hernández for allowing the appointments to go through. "It was absolutely unacceptable for [Hernández] to proceed with the appointment, no matter what the National Assembly would have said," Rodríguez told me. "You are the attorney general. You have duties. You can't do something that goes against the [rules] of the nation . . . If somebody in the whole world knew that that was wrong, it was him. I am 110 percent against Maduro and against Chávez," Rodríguez continued, adding his "intention was not to make a scandal out of this, but to make a warning as private as possible." "Once you see the case and the things that Hernández did, or allowed the National Assembly to do, you can see that it was of such a benefit to Crystallex, that for the judges it became a clear case," Rodríguez lamented. Most shockingly, Rodríguez revealed to Venezuelan lawmakers that Hernández had testified as an "expert witness" in the case, on Crystallex's behalf, before taking over as Guaidó's "Attorney General." In April of 2017, Hernández was asked to help prove CITGO was in fact an

160 Anya Parampil, "The Citgo Conspiracy: Opposition Figures Accuse Guaidó Offcials of 'Scam' to Liquidate Venezuela's Most Prized International Asset," *Grayzone*, September 3, 2019, https://thegrayzone.com/2019/09/03/the-citgo-conspiracy-opposition-figures-accuse-guaido-officials-of-scam-to-liquidate-venezuelas-most-prized-international-asset/, accessed December 29, 2019.

"alter ego" of the Venezuelan government in order to justify Crystallex's claim against the company. Hernández would go on to help prove that very aspect of Crystallex's argument through his actions as Guaidó's top legal advisor. And within months of Hernández's appointment to "Attorney General," Crystallex's case against CITGO was magically closed. Outraged lawmakers told Rodríguez that they had never been notified of Hernández's apparent conflict of interest during his rushed confirmation process.

Hernández has since tried to claim he "never analyzed the alter ego thesis nor its merits."[161] Yet even Crystallex itself noted in a March 2019 court filing that "before assuming his current position, José Ignacio Hernández—Special Counsel to the Venezuelan National Assembly tasked with evaluating creditor claims against Venezuela—provided expert testimony supporting Crystallex's alter ego arguments."[162] What's more, Hernández had also offered witness testimony in yet another "alter ego" case against CITGO. In 2013, Ohio glassmaker Owens Illinois paid Hernández $163,720 for expert testimony he provided the company in its legal effort to take shares in CITGO as compensation for money owed by the Venezuela's government.[163] "[The Crystallex decision] has a lot of implications because it completely opens the door to the whole list of companies that are suing PdVSA" for a

161 Andrés RojasJiménez, "José Ignacio Hernández: He SidoDifamado y Sometido Al EscarnioPúblico," *Hispano Post*, August 9, 2019, www.hispanopost.com/he-sido-difamado-y-sometido-al-escarnio-pubico-segun-el-codigo-penal, accessed December 29, 2019.

162 *Crystallex International Corp. vs. Bolivarian Republic of Venezuela.*

163 *OI European Group B.V. vs. RepúblicaBolivariana de Venezuela*, ICSID case no. ARB/11/25, Award, March 10, 2015, http://icsid2les.worldbank.org/icsid/ICSIDBLOBS/OnlineAwards/C1800/DC5643_Sp.pdf, accessed December 29, 2019.

slice of CITGO, Rodríguez told me.

Yet CITGO's peril did not end with vultures such as Crystallex and Owens Illinois. In 2016, Venezuela, led by Maduro, negotiated a debt swap with U.S. bondholders which saw Caracas offer up a 50.1 percent stake in CITGO in exchange for a line of credit for his cashstarved government. Venezuela made regular payments on that debt, scheduled to be paid off entirely in January 2020, until the United States recognized Guaidó's authority.[164] While Guaidó's representatives did make one payment on the 2020 debt in May of 2019, his administration began to change its tune as an October 2019 payment deadline approached. In mid-October, the Guaidó-controlled National Assembly passed a resolution which declared the debt to be illegal.[165] Lawmakers argued the original agreement which placed CITGO up as collateral was invalid because it had never been submitted to the National Assembly for authorization, despite the fact that PdVSA debt agreements have never been subject to such approval. The National Assembly tweeted out the resolution shortly after 5:30 p.m. EST on October 15, following a day of discussion.[166] Bizarrely, Deputy Vice President Stalin

[164] "Fitch Places CITGO's Ratings on Negative Watch," *Business Wire*, September 22, 2016, www.businesswire.com/news/home/20160922005991/en/Fitch-Places-CITGOs-Ratings-Negative-Watch, accessed December 29, 2019.

[165] Lucas Koerner, "Venezuela's Opposition Declares PDVSA 2020 Bond Void, Nixes Payment," *Venezuelanalysis*, October 17, 2019, https://venezuelanalysis.com/news/14695, accessed December 29, 2019.

[166] Asamblea Nacional de Venezuela (@AsambleaVE), "#Acuerdo que autoriza al ciudadano Presidente (E) de la República para que procesadacon nombramiento de los miembros de la junta de administración AD-HOC," Twitter post, October 15, 2019, 5:34 p.m., https://twitter.com/AsambleaVE/status/1184221078366892032, accessed December 29, 2019.

González's signature appeared on the document despite having been photographed mere hours later in Washington, D.C., watching a Nationals baseball game from expensive third baseline seats. How exactly he managed to travel from Caracas and into those DC Nationals seats in such a seemingly impossible amount of time was unknown.[167] Also unclear was why the National Assembly would declare the debt to be illegal so late in the game, with a looming payment only weeks away—and after having already made a payment on the loan, seemingly validating its legitimacy, in May. Regardless of their thought process, by mid-October it became increasingly clear that Guaidó would default on the loan, which would in turn allow U.S. creditors to foreclose upon their majority stake in CITGO.

CITGO's impending destruction was prevented by an eleventh-hour intervention by the U.S. Treasury Department. As a result of U.S. sanctions, all Venezuelan assets, including CITGO, are currently frozen. In order for Crystallex or Owens Illinois or the 2020 bondholders, or anyone else for that matter, to cash in on their claim in CITGO, Treasury's Office of Foreign Asset Control (OFAC) would have to issue a special waiver granting them permission to breach U.S. financial restrictions. While the Treasury had previously issued such a waiver, known as a "general license," in the case of the 2020 bondholders, it announced an update to the measure just hours before Guaidó was scheduled to default on the loan. On October 24, the Treasury temporarily suspended

[167] Alvarez, Author Alfredo, Author David Milanes, Author Dayana Villalobos Dimare, and Author Andres Finol, "Stalin Gonzalez y Su Presencia En El 4to Juego De La NLCS," *Con Las Bases Llenas*, October 22, 2019, https://con-lasbasesllenas.com/el-caso-del-diputado-stalin-gonzalez-y-su-presencia-en-el-4to-juego-de-la-nlcs/, accessed December 29, 2019.

its exemption for the bondholders, essentially delaying a CITGO foreclosure until January 2020.[168] In announcing the change, OFAC encouraged the Guaidó regime to strike a deal with creditors in order to avoid a foreclosure on CITGO. "To the extent an agreement may be reached on proposals to restructure or refinance payments due to the holders of the [debt], additional licensing requirements may apply," OFAC stated, adding it "would have a favorable licensing policy toward such an agreement."[169]

At this point, it is impossible to predict CITGO's fate—though it is unlikely that Guaidó representatives will work out a deal with creditors. Whether or not U.S. bondholders, Crystallex, Owens Illinois, or other interested parties with pending legal fights against CITGO walk away with the largest slice of the refinery, what is consistently clear are the beneficiaries of U.S. sanction policy: the Moloch of U.S. capital and industry. If when, for example, bondholders move to foreclose upon their 50.1 percent claim in CITGO, it is not as though they will simply take ownership of that portion of the company. Rather, that half will be liquidated—sold off on the market—in order to pay back the creditors in cash. At that point industry titans will have the chance to purchase CITGO's assets and expand their share of the oil market.[170]

168 US Department of the Treasury, "Issuance of Amended Venezuela-Related General License 5A and Frequently Asked Questions," last updated October 24, 2019, www.treasury.gov/resource-center/sanctions/ofac-enforcement/pages/20191024_33.aspx, accessed December 29, 2019.

169 US Department of the Treasury, "595. What Does Venezuela-Related General License 5A Authorize?" last updated February 18, 2020, www.treasury.gov/resourcecenter/faqs/Sanctions/Pages/faq_other.aspx#595, accessed December 29, 2019.

170 Parampil, "The Citgo Conspiracy."

Industry competitors include ExxonMobil—the former employer of Guaidó's "ambassador" to the United States, Carlos Vecchio. Vecchio is a tool of U.S. industry whose career had been carefully managed by U.S. government entities seeking regime change in his country.[171] Despite presenting himself as a rising star in Venezuela's opposition, it turned out that Vecchio entered the political arena in 2007, only after Hugo Chávez successfully drove his employer at the time, ExxonMobil, out of the country. Up until that point, Vecchio had worked as a tax lawyer, leading Exxon's legal fight against the Chávez government for several years. It was only Exxon's forced exit from Venezuela (along with a series of U.S. government-funded scholarships and fellowships to study at Georgetown, Harvard, and Yale) that gave birth to Vecchio the politician and eventual "ambassador." Vecchio worked as a close ally of Hernández throughout the Crystallex saga. When news broke in Caracas of Hernández's relationship with Crystallex after the July ruling, Vecchio quickly leaped to his colleague's defense. Hernández eventually produced a document which he claimed proved he had "recused" himself from the Crystallex case back in March. Yet the so-called "recusal letter" had been addressed not to "President" Guaidó, but to Vecchio, and an analysis of the document's metadata revealed it had been created in July, not March.[172]

The shady conduct of Vecchio and Hernández, two U.S.-based Venezuelan coup officials, explains why even opponents

171 Anya Parampil and Diego Sequera, "From Exxon to 'Ambassador': How Carlos Vecchio Became Venezuela's Top Coup Lobbyist," *Grayzone*, June 18, 2019, https://thegrayzone.com/2019/06/18/exxon-ambassador-carlos-vecchio-venezuela-coup-lobbyist/, accessed December 29, 2019.

172 José Ignacio Hernández to Carlos Vecchio, March 13, 2019. This letter is analyzed in Parampil, "The Citgo Conspiracy."

of the Maduro government have started to question the true motive of Guaidó "officials." Whatever remains of their questionable political legitimacy back in Venezuela will certainly evaporate if CITGO is liquidated under their watch. As Guaidó's coup flops back at home, it becomes increasingly clear that neither Vecchio nor Hernández will ever serve a tangible government in Venezuela. Then again, if their true allegiances have always been to Washington and Wall Street, then why would they even want to return home? Did they ever truly believe they would change the situation on the ground in Caracas, or was taking control of Venezuela's international assets enough of a victory? For whom do these men truly work: the Venezuelan people or U.S. capital? Their undisclosed professional pasts and actions as "representatives" of the U.S.-recognized coup regime offer a disturbingly obvious answer.

A UNIPOLAR POWER CLINGS TO ITS CONTROL

For the United States, financial sanctions are a means through which to achieve its political objective of overthrowing governments, like that in Caracas, that continue to resist its dominance. After the fall of the Berlin Wall "everything indicated that it was going to become a unipolar world, that was going to be ruled by Washington and by the European countries allied with Washington," Venezuelan Foreign Minister Jorge Arreaza explained to me during an interview in his Caracas office in February of 2019, less than a month after the United States initiated a coup attempt against his government. "It didn't happen. No—other poles began to be forged."[173]

[173] Anya Parampil, "Venezuela's Foreign Minister on the 'Failed' Coup

According to Arreaza, the current battle between Washington and Caracas represents "the epicenter of a historical dispute" between "the right of free peoples and nations to exist, as opposed to accepting, with resignation, being simple domains of the American empire, enslaved to the service of [capital]."[174]

As demonstrated by the U.S. president's own words, that historical dispute is defined as a conflict between capitalism and socialism. "To those who would try to impose socialism on the United States, we again deliver a very simple message: America will never be a socialist country," Trump proclaimed before an audience of "Make America Great Again" (MAGA) hat-wearing Venezuelan exiles during a rally at Miami's Florida International University in February 2019. To fulfill his vow, Trump is working with international financial capital to openly sabotage Venezuela's once-thriving economy. U.S. sanctions have already allowed foreign financial institutions and the Treasury Department to siphon off billions of dollars' worth of the country's assets in broad daylight. While the U.N.-recognized government led by Maduro continues to control the country's military, borders, and ministries, sanctions have succeeded in cutting off Venezuela's access to its own, internationally stored wealth. This blatant piracy was enabled by the U.S. unrivaled strength as an empire. Unable and unwilling to commit U.S. troops to conventional forms

---

and Building a New Non-Aligned Movement," *Grayzone*, February 19, 2019, https://thegrayzone.com/2019/02/19/venezuelas-foreign-minister-on-the-failed-coup-and-building-a-new-non-aligned-movement/, accessed December 29, 2019.

174 Jorge Arreaza M (@Jaarreaza), "Aquínuestrare}exión sobre la Disputa Estructural que ha marcado y marcará el destino de Venezuela," Twitter post, June 19, 2019, 11:34 a.m., https://twitter.com/jaarreaza/status/1141368625787559942?s=08, accessed December 29, 2019.

of combat, Washington now opts to strangle its enemies by leaning on an international financial system that forms its foundation as an imperial force. At the core of U.S. empire lies the beating heart of international finance capital. For this reason, sanctions, or more accurately, "financial terrorism," is the ultimate tool of imperialism. For this reason, only the creation of an international system based on alternatives to U.S.-ruled financial institutions and the U.S. dollar can adequately challenge Washington's imperial power, and ensure the right of free and independent people of the world to exist.

ELLIOTT ABRAMS, WEAPONIZED

Belén Fernández

In January 2019, shortly after Juan Guaidó auto-proclaimed himself interim president of Venezuela—to the delight of Donald Trump & Co.—the United States appointed a special envoy to the country. In the words of U.S. Secretary of State Mike Pompeo, the new appointee was a "seasoned, principled, and tough-minded foreign policy veteran," whose "passion for the rights and liberties of all peoples" ensured that he would be "a true asset to our mission to help the Venezuelan people fully restore democracy and prosperity to their country."[175]

For those of us accustomed to the United States' signature perversions of language (e.g., the annihilation of Iraq = "Iraqi Freedom," the Israeli slaughter of Palestinians =

175 Ray Sanchez, "US Special Envoy for Venezuela Has Long, Controversial History in Latin America," *CNN*, January 26, 2019, https://edition.cnn.com/2019/01/26/americas/elliott-abrams-nezuela-special-envoy-career/index.html, accessed June 9, 2020; Reuters, "Former U.S. Diplomat Abrams to Lead Efforts on Venezuela," January 25, 2019, www.reuters.com/article/us-venezuela-politics-usa-abrams/former-u-s-diplomat-abrams-to-lead-efforts-on-venezuela-idUSKCN1PJ2IC, accessed June 9, 2020.

"self-defense"), the identity of the envoy should perhaps have come as no surprise: Elliott Abrams, Iran-Contra convict and longtime enemy of democracy in Latin America and beyond. Indeed, Pompeo's celebration of Abrams' alleged "passion" for rights and liberties is reminiscent of Abrams' own insistence that Guatemalan dictator Efraín Ríos Montt had "brought considerable progress" in the field of human rights—or the time he recalled the Ronald Reagan administration's blood-soaked record in El Salvador as one "of fabulous achievement."[176]

For the past 40 years, Abrams has displayed his "principled" foreign policy approach by participating at the forefront of U.S. abridgements of rights and liberties across the Global South.[177] In one instance of particularly grotesque euphemism, Abrams commenced his stint as Reagan's assistant secretary of state for human rights and humanitarian affairs precisely one day after the notorious 1981 massacre of up to 1,200 people in the Salvadoran village of El Mozote by the U.S.-trained and funded Atlacatl Battalion.[178] His

---

176 Elisabeth Malkin, "Trial on Guatemalan Civil War Carnage Leaves Out U.S. Role," *New York Times*, May 16, 2013, www.nytimes.com/2013/05/17/world/americas/trial-on-guatemalan-civil-war-carnage-leaves-out-us-role.html, accessed June 9, 2020; Guy Gugliota and Douglas Farah, "12 Years of Tortured Truth on El Salvador," *Washington Post*, March 21, 1993, www.washingtonpost.com/archive/politics/1993/03/21/12-years-of-tortured-truth-on-el-salvador/9432bb6f-fbd0-4b18-b254-29caa919dc98/, accessed June 9, 2020.

177 Jon Schwarz, "Elliott Abrams, Trump's Pick to Bring Democracy to Venezuela, Has Spent His Life Crushing Democracy," *The Intercept*, January 30, 2019, https://theintercept.com/2019/01/30/elliott-abrams-venezuela-coup/, accessed June 9, 2020.

178 Óscar Martínez and Juan José Martínez, *The Hollywood Kid: The Violent Life and Violent Death of an MS-13 Hitman* (New York: Verso

official dedication to human rights and humanitarianism notwithstanding, Abrams promptly set about denying that any such massacre had ever happened. After all, public knowledge of such episodes could jeopardize ongoing U.S. financial support for rightwing forces in El Salvador, bent on terrorizing the nation in the name of anti-communism.

Former U.S. ambassador to El Salvador, Robert White, wrote in a 1980 classified cable assessing the country's incipient civil war: "The daily total of dead, many among them teenagers bearing marks of brutal torture, result from right-wing terrorism."[179] The economic motives behind the conflict were not lost on the American diplomat: "In El Salvador the rich and powerful have systematically defrauded the poor and denied eighty percent of the people any voice in the affairs of their country," a situation that had brought "decades of oppression and a studied refusal on the part of the elite to make any concessions to the masses."[180]

Some 75,000 Salvadorans ultimately perished during the twelve-year civil war, with the vast majority of crimes attributed to the U.S.-backed state, allied paramilitary formations, and death squads.[181] In addition to portraying this outcome as a "fabulous achievement," Abrams defended Roberto d'Aubuisson, mastermind behind the assassination of Salvadoran Archbishop Óscar Romero. According to Abrams, d'Aubuisson was not an extremist because to be an

Books, 2019), 302.

179 Raymond Bonner, *Weakness and Deceit: America and El Salvador's Dirty War* (New York: O/R Books, 2016), 48.

180 Ibid., 47–8.

181 United States Institute of Peace, *From Madness to Hope: The 12-Year War in El Salvador: Report of the Commission on the Truth for El Salvador*, January 26, 2001, www.usip.org/sites/default/@les/@le/ElSalvador-Report.pdf, accessed June 9, 2020.

extremist "you would have to be engaged in murder."[182]

This abuse of logic was entirely in line with the imperial lexicon, which defines "extremism" as something only exhibited by America's enemies and international "democracy" as the province of a far-right wing, obsequious to U.S. corporate interests. From lauding Ríos Montt's human rights "progress"—in the context of a devastating war that killed over 200,000 Guatemalans, with the state found to be responsible for no less than 93 percent of human rights violations—to aiding and abetting a Contra war against Nicaragua in the 1980s, Abrams' record in Central America alone would appear to make him a strong contender for the "extremist" label himself.[183]

Regarding the Contra war, historian Roxanne Dunbar-Ortiz writes in her memoir *Blood on the Border* that, despite Abrams' upbeat prediction that "'when history is written the Contras will be folk heroes' . . . [n]o one remembers the Contras as anything but mercenaries of the United States, except perhaps for Abrams and his small circle of neoconservatives."[184] Some 50,000 Nicaraguans were killed in this war, but Abrams presented himself as the preeminent victim. In 1991, he was convicted for withholding information

182 Raymond Bonner, "Time for a U.S. Apology to El Salvador," *The Nation*, April 15, 2016, www.thenation.com/article/archive/time-for-a-us-apology-to-el-salvador/, accessed June 9, 2020.

183 United States Institute of Peace, *Truth Commission: Guatemala*, February1, 1997, www.usip.org/publications/1997/02/truth-commission-guatemala, accessed June 9, 2020; Noam Chomsky, "Teaching Nicaragua a Lesson" (excerpt from *What Uncle Sam Really Wants*, 1992), https://chomsky.info/unclesam08/, accessed June 9, 2020.

184 Roxanne Dunbar-Ortiz, *Blood on the Border: A Memoir of the Contra War* (Norman: University of Oklahoma Press, 2016), 264.

from Congress about his role in Iran-Contra, including an incident when he gave the Sultan of Brunei an incorrect Swiss bank account number and the Contras missed out on a $10 million donation.[185] His conviction entailed 100 hours of community service, two years of probation, and a $50 fine. Although Abrams was pardoned the following year by George H.W. Bush, he conveyed his continuing indignation in a book titled *Undue Process: A Story of How Political Differences Are Turned into Crimes.*[186] In one memorable line, he transcribes his train of thought vis-à-vis the prosecution: "You miserable, filthy bastards, you bloodsuckers!"[187]

How do we balance 100 hours of community service with the bayoneting of small children at El Mozote?[188] Furthermore, criminalization of political differences seems to be what the Cold War was about in the first place—with Abrams one of the characters in charge of criminalizing and punishing those who, like in El Salvador, might have wanted a "voice in the affairs of their country," or who might have

185 Associated Press, "Iran-Contra Hearings; Brunei Regains $10 Million," July 22, 1987, www.nytimes.com/1987/07/22/world/iran-contra-hearings-brunei-regains-10-million.html, accessed June 9, 2020.

186 George Lardner, Jr., "Abrams Sentence to 2 Years' Probation, Fined $50," *Washington Post*, November 16, 1991, www.washingtonpost.com/archive/politics/1991/11/16/abrams-sentenced-to-2-years-probation-fined-50/b1f480ad-f16c-4c8c-8787-e910888611c4/, accessed June 9, 2020.

187 Joseph Finder, "Righteous Indignation," *New York Times*, November 15, 1992, www.nytimes.com/1992/11/15/books/righteous-indignation.html, accessed June 9, 2020.

188 Micah Uetricht and Branko Marketic, "Remember El Mozote," *Jacobin*, December 12, 2016, https://jacobinmag.com/2016/12/el-mozote-el-salvador-war-reagan-atlacatl-massacre, accessed June 9, 2020.

opposed the misery resulting from the U.S. model, or who might have simply been caught in the crossfire.

Yet, Abrams' past hardly ever gets in his way. Since 1981, he has held a number of posts across various administrations, many of them involving the terms "human rights" and "democracy." One of the few U.S. politicians to contest his appointment as special envoy to Venezuela was Congresswoman Ilhan Omar (D-MN), who, during a February 2019 House Foreign Affairs subcommittee hearing, confronted him about his track record of deceit. Recalling Abrams' dismissal of reports of the El Mozote massacre as "communist propaganda," Omar reminded him how U.S.-trained troops had "bragged about raping a 12-year-old girl, girls, before they killed them." In response to her question of whether he continued to stand by his whole "fabulous achievement" assessment, Abrams declared: "From the day that President [José Napoleón] Duarte was elected in a free election [in 1984], to *this* day, El Salvador has been a democracy. That's a fabulous achievement." With his declaration, Abrams ignored the fact that the election in question was not at all free, or that current Salvadoran "democracy" is characterized by corruption, widespread poverty, and extraordinary violence. That more members of the U.S. political establishment have declined to confront Abrams on his rank deceit might call into question the state of U.S. democracy itself.

On the Venezuelan front, Abrams condemns late President Hugo Chávez for being one of those world leaders that "abused . . . power" in order to "bring their country's fragile democracy to an end."[189] In fact, Abrams is reported

[189] Elliott Abrams, *Realism and Democracy: American Foreign Police after the Arab Spring* (Cambridge: Cambridge University Press,

to have been a key player in the 2002 coup attempt against Chávez.[190] By appointing Abrams, the Trump administration clarifies its policy in relation to Venezuela: loudly proclaim the values of democracy and human rights, in order to justify and support brutal violence against poor Venezuelans who support their government.[191]

In a study for the Center for Economic and Policy Research, Mark Weisbrot and Jeffrey Sachs find that asphyxiating U.S. sanctions have "reduced the public's caloric intake, increased disease and mortality (for both adults and infants), and displaced millions of Venezuelans who fled the country as a result of the worsening economic depression and hyperinflation."[192] Predictably, the poorest and most vulnerable people have been disproportionately harmed.

During a November 27, 2019, press briefing in Washington, Abrams praised the sanctions and referenced "plans to reinforce the effort . . . [W]e will continue our sanctions program and try to make it work better and better." As he portrayed the situation, sanctions were not at all to blame for Venezuela's plight; the United States was simply "try[ing] as best we can to help ameliorate the humanitarian situation while we work for [regime] change in Venezuela."[193]

2019), 152.

190 Ed Vulliamy, "Venezuela Coup Linked to Bush Team," *Guardian*, April 21, 2002, www.theguardian.com/world/2002/apr/21/usa.venezuela, accessed June 9, 2020.

191 Schwarz, "Elliott Abrams, Trump's Pick to Bring 'Democracy' to Venezuela."

192 Mark Weisbrot and Jeffrey Sachs, *Economic Sanctions as Collective Punishment: The Case of Venezuela* (Washington, D.C.: Center for Economic and Policy Research, April 2019), http://cepr.net/images/stories/reports/venezuela-sanctions-2019-04.pdf, accessed June 9, 2020.

193 "Special Representative for Venezuela Elliott Abrams: Special

Describing ostensible maneuvers "to restore democracy to Venezuela" and excitement about "the day when democracy has returned," Abrams warned that "the gravy train days [Venezuela] had 10 years ago are over"—referring, as the *Venezuelanalysis* website points out, to the "period when Venezuela had the highest minimum wage in Latin America and among the lowest levels of inequality."[194] Equality in Latin America is what Abrams has spent much of his career fighting.

America's "backyard" isn't the only locale that's been on the receiving end of Abrams' sadistic touch. In Iraq, he contributed to planning during the run-up to the U.S. invasion of 2003. In the Gaza Strip, he was integral to a "covert initiative . . . to provoke a Palestinian civil war," according to a 2008 *Vanity Fair* exposé.[195] In Lebanon, he testified on behalf of the Israeli military's supposed self-restraint and surgical precision in the 2006 war, which resulted in the deaths of 1,200 or so people, primarily civilians. In his 2017 testimony before a U.S. Congressional committee, Abrams reminisced about his wartime visit to Beirut with then-Secretary of State Condoleezza Rice—who described the bloodshed as the "birth pangs of a new Middle East"—when he had observed Israel's treatment of the Beirut lighthouse: "An Israeli missile had gone right through the lighthouse's top and taken out its searchlight. There was no damage to the structure, so that all

Briefing," Washington, D.C., November 27, 2019, www.state.gov/special-representative-for-venezuela-elliott-abrams-2/, accessed June 9, 2020.

194 "US Vows to 'Reinforce' Sanctions, Accuses Venezuela and Cuba of Stirring Regional 'Strife,'" *Venezuelanalysis*, November 28, 2019, https://venezuelanalysis.com/news/14734, accessed June 9, 2020.

195 David Rose, "The Gaza Bombshell," *Vanity Fair*, March 3, 2008, www.vanityfair.com/news/2008/04/gaza200804, accessed June 9, 2020.

that was needed was a new searchlight and the lighthouse would instantly be operational again."[196]

Needless to say, Lebanese people obliterated at close range by Israeli helicopters could not be put back together again; nor could the people of El Salvador, Guatemala, Iraq, and beyond.[197] Yet Abrams, himself, it seems, will forever be operational, given the clearly exorbitant demand for U.S.-inflicted "democracy" and "human rights" worldwide.

Shortly after Abrams' appointment as special envoy, U.S. investigative journalist Allan Nairn tweeted that the man who had "dismissed as 'ludicrous' the idea that even he should be subject to trial for abetting massacres . . . may now be in position to do for Venezuela what he did for Guatemala."[198] As the sanctions regime amounts to an ongoing massacre, Abrams seems to be well on his way. In the 1980s as now, killing poor people in accordance with U.S. geopolitical and financial interests—Abrams' brand of lethal "humanitarianism"—is an easy sell.

The video clip accompanying Nairn's tweet dates from 1995, when Nairn and Abrams appeared on Charlie Rose's PBS television program and Abrams cackled at length at

196 Tony Karon, "Condi in Diplomatic Disneyland," *Time*, July 26, 2006, http://content.time.com/time/world/article/0,8599,1219325,00.html, accessed June 9, 2020; Council on Foreign Relations, "The Latest Developments in Saudi Arabia and Lebanon," November 29, 2017, www.cfr.org/sites/default/files/report_pdf/Abrams HFAC Testimony 11.29.17.pdf, accessed June 9, 2020.

197 Robert Fisk, "Marwahin, 15 July 2006: The Anatomy of a Massacre," *Independent*, September 30, 2006, www.independent.co.uk/voices/commentators/@sk/marwahin-15-july-2006-the-anatomy-of-a-massacre-6231215.html, accessed June 9, 2020.

198 Allan Nairn, Twitter post, January 26, 2019, 12:29 a.m., https://twitter.com/allannairn14/status/1089032468701753344?lang=en, accessed June 9, 2020.

Nairn's suggestion that he, along with Guatemalan as well as U.S. Democratic officials, would be eligible for a "Nuremberg-style inquiry." While mass bloodshed may be a laughing matter for members of the U.S. political establishment, it will be much less funny if justice ever arrives.

VENEZUELA AND PEOPLE'S RESISTANCE AGAINST IMPERIALISM

Miguel Stédile

This statement was prepared for "Holding the Future Hostage: A Conference on Hybrid Wars, Sanctions, and Solidarity," which took place at The People's Forum on October 19, 2019. The presentation has since been edited and revised for publication.

Venezuela today plays a central role in the people's resistance against imperialism, against the U.S. offensive. Today Venezuela is the target of a new type of war that is either called asymmetric war, fourth-generation war or more simply, hybrid war.

What is this war made of? It is the combination of conventional warfare with civil insurgency. This is not new in terms of military thinking: using civilians to overthrow adversarial governments. This happened, for instance, in the Spanish Civil War, with the so-called fifth column. We had it in the form of the German resistance to Nazism, and in various irregular forms of war, of civil wars. The novelty now is the use of high-tech social networks, of a powerful web of non-governmental organizations, and think tanks, to articulate the background in which this hybrid war is developed.

Why is Venezuela the epicenter of this hybrid war? Why is Venezuela the target? Latin America has been the target of an offensive by the U.S. in recent years. This offensive has taken place differently in each country. It is linked to three basic factors.

The first factor: we are experiencing a reorganization of world geopolitics. From World War II until the early 1990s, we had a polarized world. The Cold War world was dissolved with the end of the Soviet Union and the rise of U.S. hegemony and the hegemony of neoliberalism. This scenario is now changing as we see China emerging as a new political force, either by itself or in its coalition with Russia. The rise of China expresses a new dispute over natural resources such as mineral wealth and oil, alongside a new dispute for trade control in Eurasia, North Africa, and the Pacific, best expressed in the New Silk Road project, a Chinese-Russian partnership. This poses China's rise to world power, as a global player that should likely become the largest economy in the world in the coming years. What world scenario will we have in this context? A scenario that splits power between the United States and China, or a scenario of China surpassing the United States. These scenarios are being disputed at the moment.

The second factor: we are also experiencing a wide and prolonged crisis in the international financial system, which began strongly in 2008, hitting hardest the core of the capitalist system in the United States and Europe. Remember the banks going bankrupt in countries like Greece, Portugal, and Iceland. This crisis has not yet been resolved. On the contrary, it is a characteristic of capital in its financial monopoly for these crises to repeat themselves more frequently. Only now, these crises are hitting the peripheral countries harder. The international financial system is unable to resolve its own crisis because the origin of the crisis is in the very nature of the system. The capitalist system is being organized and driven by financial capital, by speculative capital, fictitious capital, interest-bearing capital.

These are expressions of capital that do not generate wealth, reproducing themselves without creating a real material basis, without generating jobs, without circulating merchandise. They are based only on speculation. Hence the name speculative capital, or fictitious capital, because it increasingly loses its real base. It is therefore unable to resolve the crisis of capitalism. The United States, as the biggest player in the international financial system, is the most affected by this crisis.

The third factor: in Latin America we have had a wave of progressive governments in recent years, as in Brazil, Argentina, Uruguay, Venezuela, Ecuador, and Bolivia. Even those that were not left wing were at least more sovereign, more autonomous. In stark contrast with the U.S. government, they were building alternative paths to exert their sovereignty. For the last few years we have been experiencing a new U.S. offensive mobilized by these three factors: the U.S. is in dispute with China; it is weakened by the crisis in the international financial system; and it needs to regain control of Latin American territory.

Because of these three scenarios, the U.S., above all under the Trump administration, has begun to attack Latin America either more violently, or using more subtle ways. It has endorsed democratically elected anti-left governments, as we have had in Peru, Chile, and Argentina. It has also set up *coups d'état*, as we had in Honduras, Paraguay, and Brazil, and attempts to destabilize countries like Venezuela.

Why is Venezuela the epicenter of this dispute? First of all, for its natural assets.

Venezuela has one of the largest (if not the largest) oil reserves in the world, above that of Saudi Arabia. It becomes necessary for the U.S. to try to control this energy source, so as to have a source of energy available in the event of a U.S. attack on Iran. A U.S. attack on Iran would destabilize the entire Middle East energy source and organization. It would unbalance the market, and Venezuela would then play a reserve role for the U.S., if it were under its control. Venezuela has also been the toughest progressive and left-wing trench for sovereignty in Latin America, since the Hugo Chávez government, a government that has not only regained self-esteem and dignity for its people—a people who had before lived in a despoiled, exploited state—but also imposed itself, in a sovereign way, on the international scene. Through the Bolivarian Alliance for the Peoples of Our Americas, Venezuela tried to build a front of resistance and articulation while contributing to sovereignty and resistance projects in Honduras, Cuba, and Bolivia, by establishing partnerships with other less wealthy countries, from the point of view of lacking natural resources and opportunities. This sets Venezuela as an example of rebellion or resistance that can be followed.

Thus, Venezuela is attacked in many ways. The first one, which the U.S. has used in Cuba for many years, and used in Chile against the government of Salvador Allende, is the economic blockade. This prevents Venezuela from being able to acquire foreign exchange and establish other international relations. Internally, the Venezuelan bourgeoisie works to foster shortages its own country, by controlling the circulation of goods and food, by depleting food resources to create a climate of hostility, and, at the same time, speculating in markets against the financial system.

It is worthwhile to remember that the U.S. also prohibited Venezuela from having any kind of resistance within the financial market. For example, it blocked and banned Venezuela's cryptocurrency, the "petro." In addition, the U.S. places a whole network of nongovernmental organizations (NGOs) to act within the country as think thanks. These think tanks are financed by American corporations, such as that of Koch Industries, which support the opposition by investing in its education, training, and propaganda. There is even, as it is known, a deep relationship between Juan Guaidó with drug trafficking and paramilitaries in Colombia. Who is financing this? Where do these financial resources come from?

This ideological war characterizes the hybrid war. It is an ideological war, supported by think tanks, by NGOs. It is an ideological war fought through "soft power," with media show all over Venezuela, and on the other hand, it is a preparation for conventional war. The possibility of U.S. intervention is not ruled out, whether through pressure of protofascist governments, such as the Bolsonaro government, or the North American government itself, attempting a military intervention against the sovereign people of Venezuela.

Today, Venezuela is the last trench to avoid the total offensive of U.S. imperialism in our countries. Venezuela not only protects its sovereign interests and its people. Moreover, the appropriation of Venezuelan oil is crucial for the U.S. to have enough reserves for an invasion adventure in Iran. In no way can we allow Venezuela to face this challenge alone. It is essential not only to express solidarity, but to exercise real and concrete actions of this solidarity. That implies fighting against misinformation and lies about the Bolivarian process and the Venezuelan people. It involves denouncing the inhumane actions of the United States government against these people.

These are the reasons for concern, and the reasons why Venezuela is the epicenter of hybrid war, the epicenter of the attack on Latin America at this time. Our duty is to defend and protect Venezuela, as we must defend and protect all nations who are struggling, all peoples who are claiming their right to sovereignty.

VENEZUELA:
COMMUNES AGAINST SANCTIONS

George Ciccariello-Maher

In Latin America, the dialectic of history has once again been thrown violently into reverse. This is nothing new, of course: a half-century ago, the region functioned as a brutal incubator for neoliberal economics, imposed through counterinsurgency and dictatorship and proving yet again that there is nothing free about the "free market." But for every action there is an equal and opposite reaction, and while social forces are not physical laws, the revolutionary energy weakened and dispersed during the neoliberal offensive was not destroyed entirely. In those spaces abandoned by the state and capital, grassroots experiments in democratic, communal self-management spread. And in zones of confrontation, this Gramscian war of position became a war of maneuver where explosive resistance and the repressive "whip of the counter-revolution" entered into a mutually reinforcing spiral.[199]

It was therefore no surprise that Latin America would

[199] Antonio Gramsci, *The Gramsci Reader: Selected Writings, 1916–1935* (New York: NYU Press, 2000), 222–30.

swing so quickly from incubator of neoliberalism to incubator of revolution, but here we are again, the pendulum pitching its full weight against us. Headlines about economic crisis, corruption scandals, and the long-foretold demise of that variegated leftist project known as the "Pink Tide" conceal coups (however "constitutional" or "soft"), a return to counterinsurgent warfare, and the rise of a new fascism across Latin America. Jair Bolsonaro embodies this shift even if he does not lead it—we would not grant this petit-fascist even so dubious an honor. In Brazil, collapsing global commodity prices provoked a recession while internal tension between state leadership and grassroots sectors weakened the left's capacity to mobilize, allowing the right to appropriate the language of anti-corruption, remove one leader and imprison another, and finally elect a fascist under the guise of "democracy." Variations of this script have played out across the region, fracturing the already tense unity of left-wing forces in the region and weakening a project that was always more than the sum of its parts.

In Venezuela, the situation is dire. Economic crisis has turned into economic catastrophe, the black market for the U.S. dollar swirling with all the destructive force of a maelstrom at the heart of the economy and throwing off the most dangerous of debris: corruption, smuggling, hoarding, black market activity, currency speculation. According to recent numbers from the Venezuelan Central Bank, inflation surpassed 130,000 percent in 2018, and by some estimates, up to 3 million Venezuelans have left the country.[200] For this, there

200 Valentina Sánchez, "Inflación venezolana superó el 130.000%

is plenty of blame to go around. The years since 2012 have seen a perfect storm of the intentional and unintentional, of falling oil prices, the death of Hugo Chávez, brutal aggression from the domestic opposition and the United States, and inaction by the government of Nicolás Maduro to correct a distorted currency control system—each element entering into a punishing feedback loop.

But there should be no doubt about one thing: that the single factor pushing the Venezuelan economy over the edge has been U.S. sanctions, and that the slide from crisis to catastrophe has been no less than intentional. Too often, however, we on the left treat sanctions solely as a question of foreign policy: imposed by governments and resisted by international solidarity activists. The reality, however, is that the sanctions, their impact, and our collective fightback begins with the domestic Venezuelan grassroots revolutionary movements that have coalesced in the directly democratic organs of popular participation and production

al final de 2018, según cifras oficiales," *France 24*, May 30, 2020, www.france24.com/es/20190529-in3acionbanco-central-venezuela-130000, accessed June 9, 2020. These and other figures are inescapably political. When it comes to inflation, what matters most is whether the poor can both *find* and *afford* necessary goods, but one characteristic of the economic chaos of the present is that those goods that can be found cannot be afforded, while those that are affordable cannot be found. With regard to emigration, we need to be similarly cautious: it's not always clear how such emigrants are counted, whether they include the more than a million already living overseas, or how many have or plan to return. Moreover, it is unclear how many emigrants had themselves previously *immigrated* from Colombia (a number in the millions) to be naturalized as Venezuelan (many hundreds of thousands at least). And finally, there are those self-professed "exiles" and reactionary conspirators to whom the only response is: *good riddance.*

known as communes. These communes stand today as a living alternative, not only to U.S. sanctions and threats of invasion, but also to long-term oil dependency, enmeshment in global capitalism, and the crisis these have wrought in the present. The answer to hybrid warfare is therefore not simply "hands off Venezuela," but *more* hands-on deck building a grassroots socialist alternative to capitalism in Venezuela and beyond.

Here we should be absolutely clear: sanctions are *murder*. All talk of "targeted" or "surgical" sanctions to punish the Maduro government while sparing the population is a cynical lie, and as I will show, the liars know very well that they are lying. These murderous lies began not with Donald Trump, but with Barack Obama, who absurdly declared Venezuela "an unusual and extraordinary threat to the national security and foreign policy of the United States" in 2015. Obama imposed sanctions on a handful of individuals, but as is often the case, individual sanctions are also signals to investors, and capital and finance tend to over-comply to such orders:

> Financial institutions increasingly turned away from Venezuela after March 2015, as they saw the risks of lending to a government that the United States was increasingly determined to topple—and, as the economy worsened, looked more likely to succeed in doing so. The Venezuelan private sector was cut off from vital access to credit, which contributed to the unprecedented, indeed almost unbelievable, 80 percent drop in imports over the past six years, which has devastated this import-dependent economy.[201]

[201] Mark Weisbrot, "Trump's Other 'National Emergency': Sanctions that Kill Venezuelans," *The Nation*, February 28, 2019, www.

In the inimitable words of Vijay Prashad, "Obama forged the spear; Trump has thrown it at the heart of Venezuela."[202]

This spear is deadly indeed. The report by the Center for Economic and Policy Research, co-authored by economists Mark Weisbrot and Jeffrey Sachs confirms what many on the ground already know: that in the neoliberal lexicon of the twenty-first century, to "sanction" is to kill. In August 2017, Trump imposed a vicious new sanctions package that blocked Venezuelan access to U.S. financial markets, effectively preventing any debt restructuring even remotely involving U.S. banks, and blocking Venezuelan access to funds from its U.S. affiliate, CITGO. The contours of the ensuing cycle are as follows: without money to produce oil there is no money to import food and medicine, much less to invest in producing more oil. Without financing for infrastructure and to purchase diluents and other chemical inputs, Venezuelan oil production went into free-fall immediately after sanctions were imposed.

Weisbrot and Sachs estimate that the 2017 sanctions cost Venezuela an astonishing $6 billion within a year, more than Venezuela spent in 2018 for *all imports* of food and medicine combined. It is no surprise, then, that these "targeted" sanctions had a far broader impact, and that those hardest hit would be the people, not the government. The sanctions, they demonstrate, undermined public health through a pincer movement of decreased nutrition alongside increased

thenation.com/article/venezuela-sanctions-emergency/, accessed June 9, 2020.

202 Vijay Prashad, "The Plot to Kill Venezuela," *Salon*, May 17, 2019, www.salon.com/2019/05/17/the-plot-to-kill-venezuela_partner/, accessed June 9, 2020.

disease—all disproportionately impacting Venezuela's poorest.[203] All told, Weisbrot and Sachs set the death toll from sanctions at 40,000 in late 2017 and 2018 alone—almost certainly a low estimate, with hundreds of thousands more at continued risk due to lack of access to imported medicines, HIV antiretrovirals, dialysis, and treatment for cancer, diabetes, and hypertension. And according to former Spanish prime minister José Luis Rodríguez Zapatero, no friend of Maduro, the mass exodus often leveraged as evidence against the government has everything to do with sanctions: "As always occurs with economic sanctions that create a financial blockade, in the last instance it is definitely not a government that pays the price, but the citizens, the people."[204]

Trump's 2017 sanctions were just the beginning, however. In January 2019, the Venezuelan opposition unleashed a full-fledged coup attempt with opposition benchwarmer Juan Guaidó at its head. But despite support from the Venezuelan opposition, the Latin American right, and the Trump administration, and despite the economic chaos tearing Venezuela apart, the Bolivarian Revolution showed an unexpected resilience among the grassroots and the military. Guaidó's coup faltered before it had even begun,

203 Mark Weisbrot and Jeffrey Sachs, *Economic Sanctions as Collective Punishment: The Case of Venezuela* (Washington, D.C.: Center for Economic and Policy Research, April 2019), http://cepr.net/images/stories/reports/venezuela-sanctions-2019-04.pdf, accessed June 30, 2020.

204 "Rodríguez Zapatero vincula el éxodo de los venezolanos a las sanciones impuestas por EE.UU.," EFE, September 15, 2018, www.efe.com/efe/america/sociedad/rodriguez-zapatero-vincula-el-exodo-de-los-venezolanos-a-las-sanciones-impuestas-por-ee-uu/20000013-3750573#, accessed June 9, 2020.

but the damage was already done. Maduro's international image was severely tarnished, and the United States handed over CITGO—worth more than $7 billion—and other Venezuelan assets directly to Guaidó's Vichy regime. In other words, as everyday Venezuelans found it increasingly difficult to make ends meet, Guaidó's coup made off with *three times* what the entire country spends on food and medicine in a year. The theft didn't end there: claims soon surfaced that Guaidó's people had embezzled so-called "humanitarian aid" for lavish expenditures, all while mouthing the language of anti-corruption, and a string of further corruption cases followed.[205]

There was still more to come. Shortly after Guaidó's botched coup, the Trump administration tightened the screws on the Venezuelan people. If 2017 was a financial blockade, 2019 was an oil blockade: blocking access to the U.S. market for oil and strong-arming other countries to do the same. In January 2019, Venezuela had been exporting 700,000 barrels per day to the United States, but by March that number fell to *zero*. The results have been nothing less than catastrophic. If oil production had fallen by a third after the 2017 sanctions, it collapsed completely in 2019, falling by half again. In less than two years' time, Venezuelan oil production fell from 1.9 million barrels per day to just 740,000.[206] And in a qualitative shift, oil production was now

205 Lucas Koerner and Ricardo Vaz, "Venezuela: Guaido Embattled as Opposition Splits over New Corruption Scandal," *Venezuelanalysis*, December 5, 2019, https://venezuelanalysis.com/news/14739, accessed June 9, 2020.

206 Lucas Koerner and Ricardo Vaz, "Venezuela: Widespread Gasoline Shortages as Sanctions Take Toll on Oil Sector," *Venezuelanalysis*, May 20, 2019, https://venezuelanalysis.com/news/14500, accessed June 9, 2020.

plunging not due to the supply side (lack of financing and replacement parts), but the demand side (lack of access to markets). With nowhere to store oil inventories, Caracas was forced to dump oil inventories onto the global market at a deep discount, but even then, the United States leaned heavily on countries like India to stop buying Venezuelan oil entirely.

Moreover, the Trump regime has used every extra-legal measure possible to—in the words of one financial analyst—"make Venezuela radioactive."[207] These range from special financial advisories meant to scare off lenders, to pressure and even threats against potential trading partners. Some, like opposition economist Francisco Rodríguez, argue that such measures are "perhaps even more important" and detrimental than direct sanctions.[208] And the knock-on effects have spread virally across the economy and society as a whole, with poor Venezuelan communities struggling to maintain the flow of water as sanctions block the import of necessary pumps and parts.[209] A report published by the Venezuela Solidarity Campaign has further documented the

[207] David C. Adams and Janet Rodriguez, "US Tightens the Screws on Venezuela's Maduro with Banking Sanctions," *Univisión*, March 22, 2019, www.univision.com/univision-news/latin-america/us-tightens-the-screws-on-venezuelas-maduro-with-banking-sanctions, accessed June 9, 2020.

[208] Francisco Rodríguez, "Crude Realities: Understanding Venezuela's Economic Collapse," Venezuela Politics and Human Rights, Washington Office on Latin America (WOLA), September 20, 2018, https://venezuelablog.org/crude-realities-understanding-venezuelaseconomic-collapse, accessed June 9, 2020.

[209] Michael Fox, "US Sanctions Leave Millions of Venezuelans Without Water," *The Real News*, May 26, 2019, https://therealnews.com/stories/us-sanctions-leave-millions-of-venezuelans-without-water, accessed June 9, 2020.

blocking of insulin and anti-malarial imports and scheduled bone marrow transplants, as well as the illegal withholding of nearly $5.5 billion by global financial institutions in response to U.S. sanctions and threats.[210]

Trump's most sadistic gesture, however, has been the direct targeting of the CLAP (Local Committees for Supply and Production) program. In the face of shortages, the Venezuelan government established the CLAP program in 2016 to deliver basic food items directly to people's homes. According to opposition pollster Datanálisis, nearly 75 percent of Venezuelans, Chavista and opposition alike, benefit from CLAPs today, and while there is much to criticize—namely that they are more "supply" (of imported goods) than domestic "production"—it is no accident that the United States would target the program. Between December 2018 and May 2019, the Venezuelan government sought to eliminate the black market exchange rate and halt hyperinflation by devaluing the bolívar and eliminating preferential access to dollars. Unlike neoliberal shock therapy, however, institutions like CLAPs exist to cushion the blow for the poorest, and if the Venezuelan government opts for a more radically communist turn—as it no doubt should—it would rely on these direct distribution circuits while jumpstarting communal production. The opposition burned a CLAP warehouse during Guaidó's short-lived coup attempt and the United Sates chose to target the program because the CLAPs are "military targets."[211]

---

210 Venezuela Solidarity Campaign, "Briefing: The Effects of the Economic Blockade of Venezuela," June 2019, www.venezuelasolidarity.co.uk/wp-content/uploads/2019/ 06/ /The-effects-of-the-economic-blockade-of-Venezuela-final7359.pdf, accessed June 9, 2020.

211 "Los CLAP como objetivo de guerra: incendian galpones en el puerto de La Guaira," *Misión Verdad*, February 27, 2019, http://

The 40,000 sanctions-related deaths estimated by Weisbrot and Sachs do not even include this most recent wave of sanctions, which the authors rightly fear will prove even more devastating. Moreover, they argue that by engaging in the collective punishment of civilians, these sanctions represent a clear violation of the Geneva and Hague conventions, and are furthermore illegal under international and U.S. law. Speaking more recently on *Democracy Now*, Sachs—himself once an advocate of neoliberal "shock therapy"—was straightforward: "there is a humanitarian catastrophe, deliberately caused by the United States, by what I would say are illegal sanctions, because they are deliberately trying to bring down a government and trying to create chaos for the purpose of an overthrow of a government."[212] What is to be done? It is not enough to simply point out the inevitable human cost of sanctions, because this is *precisely the point*: to make the people suffer in the hope that they will eventually revolt against their government. If there were any doubt about this strategy, we need look no further than Trump's Secretary of State Mike Pompeo, who has spoken of tightening the "noose" around Venezuela's neck, or to another unnamed official who openly compared sanctions to Darth Vader's death grip.[213] A U.S. embassy official in Mexico

misionverdad.com/entrevistas%20/los-clap-como-objetivo-de-guerra-incendian-galpones-en-el-puerto-de-la-guaira, accessed June 9, 2020.

212 "Economist Jeffrey Sachs: U.S. Sanctions Have Devastated Venezuela & Killed over 40,000 since 2017," *Democracy Now*, May 1, 2019, www.democracynow.org/2019/5/1/economist_jeffrey_sachs_us_sanctions_have, accessed June 9, 2020.

213 Ricardo Vaz, "Venezuela: Canada Imposes Fresh Sanctions as Pompeo Vows to 'Tighten Noose,'" April 15, 2019, https://venezuelanalysis.com/news/14431, accessed June 9, 2020; Adams and Rodriguez, "US

was even more straightforward, stating that "we are seeing a total economic collapse," which means that "our policy is working."[214] Former U.S. ambassador to Venezuela William Brownfield agreed, arguing sadistically that "perhaps the best solution is to accelerate the collapse" even if it means "months or years of suffering."[215]

Here too, the consensus is bipartisan: Trump is simply expanding on a regime change project set into motion by Obama, whose own policy was hardly distinguishable from that of his predecessor, George W. Bush. In August 2019, the U.S. government froze all Venezuelan assets and doubled down on threats toward third parties. In the words of Trump's hawkish former National Security Advisor John Bolton, "We are sending a signal to third parties that want to do business with the Maduro regime: proceed with extreme caution . . . There is no need to risk your business interests with the United States." Inflation, declining in response to measures taken by the Maduro government, immediately spiked, and Venezuelan Foreign Minister Jorge Arreaza accused Trump of using sanctions to "dynamite the dialogue" between government and opposition.[216] Sanctions are a double-edged sword, however, and social unrest is an unpredictable

Tightens the Screws."

214 "Sesión informativa sobre viaje del Secretario Tillerson a Latinoamérica," January 29, 2018, https://mx.usembassy.gov/es/sesion-informativa-sobre-viaje-del-secretario-tillerson-latinoamerica/, accessed June 9, 2020.

215 "Ex embajador sugiere 'acelerar el colapso' de Venezuela," *Voz de América*, October 12, 2018, www.youtube.com/watch?v=IJBoe3AvSvc, accessed June 9, 2020.

216 Kevin Young, "Washington Intensifies Its Collective Punishment of Venezuelans," *NACLA*, August 14, 2019, https://nacla.org/news/2019/08/15/washington-intensifies-its-collective-punishment-venezuelans, accessed June 9, 2020.

quantity—we can increase the pressure, but we rarely know in which direction it will eventually escape. Specifically, the sanctions question functions today as a wedge splitting opposition forces: the radical reactionary fringe embodied by Guaidó, a poor stand-in for Leopoldo López, supports sanctions, while the bulk of the opposition—and the vast majority of the Venezuelan population—oppose them. When Guaidó failed to deliver on promises of a quick coup in January, his leverage in Washington and Caracas alike began to collapse, and it has only been downhill from there, with a string of corruption scandals and an unclear path forward chipping away at what little support he had enjoyed. When Trump later sacked Bolton, the architect of his Venezuela strategy, he may as well have fired Guaidó in the process.

Where reactionary history sees only eternal cycles, a dialectical perspective instead reveals spirals: shifting conditions, emergent self-consciousness, the persistence of radical tradition and memories of resistance, but also the forgetting and erasure that sees these gradually fade or stamped out by brutal repression. All are permanent elements of Latin American history, and all are present in Venezuela and the region today. Each turn of the spiral brings neither eternal recurrence nor inevitable progress, but only a new struggle between a left and a right transformed, a changing people confronting a world in motion.

There is no denying that recent years have seen a shift in the balance of forces away from revolutionary grassroots sectors and toward more entrenched, conservative, and corrupt elements of the state apparatus, and that economic crisis, foreign aggression, and sanctions have exacerbated this shift and fueled already endemic corruption, public and private alike. Currency speculation, hoarding and black market trading in price-controlled goods (*bachaqueo*, whose etymological derivation evokes the voracity of swarming red ants), and smuggling of domestically produced food and especially gasoline, which crosses the Colombian border as if through a massive funnel to the tune of billions of dollars a year—these all line the pockets of the already rich and well-connected bureaucrats while shelves go empty and the poor struggle to find their next meal.[217] In this context, the military has amassed undeniable political and economic clout, due in no small part to its control over smuggling routes and borders, even leveraging the creation of a special military economic zone and military-run mining corporation in the controversial Orinoco Mining Arc.

During Guaidó's failed coup, moreover, military loyalty

[217] Even prior to sanctions, an estimated 40 percent of all food either produced in or imported to Venezuela was smuggled across the Colombian border to be resold at higher prices (the rate in western Zulia State was more than 50 percent), along with the gasoline equivalent of more than 100,000 barrels of oil, costing the government almost $4 billion annually. It is revealing that even amid the sanctions-fueled catastrophe of the present, which has seen widespread shortages, food is still smuggled *out* of Venezuela for profit. Oscar Medina and Matthew Bristow, "Pocketing 1,000% Markup, Venezuelans Smuggle Out Precious Food," *Bloomberg*, February 12, 2019, www.bloomberg.com/news/articles/2019-02-12/pocketing-1-000-markup-venezuelans-smuggle-out-precious-food, accessed June 9, 2020. Of course, Colombia has never done anything at all to curb smuggling, allowing Venezuelan subsidies to feed its own neglected poor while anti-Chavista conspirators and currency speculators brazenly operate out of the border haven of Cúcuta (from where Guaidó launched his failed attempt to force fake "humanitarian aid" across the border).

was an invaluable commodity, with U.S. officials shamelessly offering to buy off any general willing to be purchased. None took the bait, thankfully, but when the military brass plays kingmaker, the grassroots suffer, and as the Chilean example makes clear, betting on military loyalty is a dangerous game for leaders as well. Corruption and expanding military power have gone hand-in-hand with a conservative agenda that has seen privatization and the repression of workers' struggles. For example, when agriculture minister Wilmar Castro Soteldo, associated with the more conservative wing of Chavismo, moved to privatize the Arroz del Alba rice factory in early 2019, workers occupied the factory, only to be arrested and held for more than two months. After public protest from social movements and even the former (more radical) agriculture minister Elías Jaua, these comuneros were eventually freed but the wave of privatizations continues unabated.[218]

What explains this shift in the balance of forces? For many on the right and even some sectors of the U.S. left, the answer comes down to a single word: Maduro. But if the years since Chávez's death have largely coincided with this shift, correlation does not mean causation, and if we know anything about Venezuelan history, it is that the causal chains involved are far too long and tangled, the dialectics at play too numerous and intermingled, to make any such easy assessments. We should not therefore be surprised to find that even the correlation doesn't hold: Maduro actually *increased* support for the network of grassroots communes in the years following Chávez's death, under the leadership

[218] Ricardo Vaz, "Venezuela: Popular Movements Secure Release of Detained Communards," *Venezuelanalysis*, April 24, 2019, https://venezuelanalysis.com/news/14441, accessed June 9, 2020.

of radical commune minister Reinaldo Iturriza. More importantly, however, to exaggerate the shift from Chávez to Maduro is to fall back into the cardinal sin of investing individuals with the power of social forces.[219]

While Chávez was about as close to a social force as any individual could hope to be, his absence also coincides with a shift in global material conditions, the collapse in commodity prices (oil very much included), bloody aggression from within and abroad, the real exhaustion and diminishing half-life of revolutionary energy, and the disintegration of the Pink Tide as a broader support network for radical experiments across the region. But the fundamental point is that these and other tendencies were already present under Chávez, and particularly the tension of tensions between constituent and constituted powers, grassroots and state which, ceteris paribus, can and has fed into the emergence of an arrogant new elite embedded within state institutions.[220] There was no single tipping point, only the constant hegemonic push-and-pull of a revolutionary struggle with no guarantees.

This is without a doubt the most difficult moment of the Bolivarian Revolution, but this has been a process with no easy moments. Why would we expect anything different? The Bolivarian process emerged not from an uninterrupted chain of victories, but from the failures, miscalculations, and crushing defeat of the Venezuelan armed struggle and from a subsequent generation of revolutionary grassroots

[219] If my books *We Created Chávez* and *Building the Commune* had a single, shared objective, it was the debunking of this myth.

[220] See the excellent book by radical sociologist Ociel Alí López, *Dale más gasolina! Chavismo, sifrinismo y burocracia* (Caracas: Fundación Andrés Bello, 2015), www.ecestaticos.com/file/a86c18609a22d4ccebb5a310ba88f870/1505112532-dale-mas-gasolina-pdf-4.pdf, accessed June 9, 2020.

movements fighting a stubborn but losing battle against the state and capital alike. It grew from a thousand failed experiments and a hundred blind alleys, from the desperate revolt and bloody repression of the 1989 Caracazo rebellion—like so many flowers sprouting atop recently fertilized mass graves. The going has *never* been easy, and when it comes to revolution, the odds are never in our favor.

The Pink Tide, that ebullient period of progressive and leftist hegemony across Latin America, may indeed be over, but the right's return to power does not mean the defeat of the left. We may instead be merely witnessing an interlude, a moment for reflection and radicalization, a tactical retreat from a state to which we owe nothing but permanent suspicion. The forces of reaction are extending their reach and sharpening their knives, but they are far from invincible. It is increasingly obvious that the Latin American right stands on feet of clay: Mauricio Macri's Argentinean intermezzo lasted four short years, and approval is collapsing for besieged right-wing governments in Brazil, Ecuador, and Colombia. Unable to defeat Evo Morales at the ballot box, the Bolivian right resorted to a coup, but between street resistance and the ham-fisted racism of the coup leaders, the story is far from over. And Mexico has bucked the regional trend by electing Andrés Manuel López Obrador, but much will depend on the perilous balancing act of pragmatism with revolutionary dynamism.

In Venezuela as elsewhere across the region, the source of that dynamism is the same: those revolutionary grassroots movements forced to walk a fine line between the state and its dissolution, between the insurrectionary *against* and the communal *for*. Here the network of communes that has expanded across the Venezuelan sociopolitical landscape over the past decade is crucial for more reasons than one. A commune brings together local organs of direct and participatory democracy (communal councils among others) with direct and communal production in which the communal parliament decides democratically what will be produced, who will produce it, how much they will be paid, and how to reinvest the surplus into the communal economy itself. As institutions of locally rooted democratic production, the communes thus provide a living, breathing alternative to the crisis of the present and to capitalist dependency writ large.

If the past century of Venezuelan history has been marked by the country's increasing dependency on oil exports and the consumer culture that cheap imports make possible, this oil/consumer dependency has also been the Achilles heel of any project for substantial change: domestic production atrophies, undermining the development of sustainable local alternatives for when oil prices inevitably drop and crisis sets in. The communes are the opposite of all this: producing what people need locally and creating a revolutionary sustainability that is not subject to the whims of the global market. And in a perverse way, the crisis and sanctions of the present have even encouraged the deepening of communal production: much like the Cuban "Special Period," people at the grassroots level have been forced to invent new and creative ways to produce those goods that can no longer be cheaply imported.

The commune is about more than mere production, however, and as former commune minister Reinaldo Iturriza often observes, the commune doesn't simply produce but is also itself produced and reproduced in revolutionary communal culture. The communes, however beaten and battered by crisis and sanctions, have come to coalesce the most intransigently revolutionary forces in Venezuelan society, those seeking not only to *preserve* but to *deepen* the Bolivarian process. They preserve it by providing its best defense against aggression from within and without: as far back as the 2002 coup, it was the most organized grassroots revolutionary elements that brought Chávez back to power, and it has been these same sectors that have saved the revolution again and again. They manage popular education and food distribution programs, they provide grassroots intelligence—the eyes and ears of the community in the battle against hoarding and corruption—and they are the backbone of an armed, grassroots militia—now millions strong—capable of resisting not only foreign invasion but also enemies within the traditional military.[221] But as I show in *Building the Commune*, the communal horizon seeks not to reinforce the state as-is, but in the words of Chávez, to "pulverize the bourgeois state" and replace it with something far different.

Today as always, the best antidote to sanctions, coups, and hybrid wars is communism. In his homage to the revolutionary struggle in El Salvador, the Venezuelan folk singer Alí Primera once wrote that "The march is slow, but it is still the march, and it is by pushing the sun that dawn approaches."[222] For the Venezuelan comuneras and comuneros continuing to struggle today, there is no alternative to this march and no expectation that it will be easy—there is only

221 Paul Dobson, "Venezuela's Civilian Militia Surpasses Target, Reaches 3.3 Million Members," *Venezuelanalysis*, December 9, 2019, https:// venezuelanalysis.com/ news/14742, accessed June 9, 2020.

222 "Dale que la marcha es lenta pero sigue siendo marcha, dale que empujando el sol se acerca la madrugada." "El Sombrero Azul," *Al Pueblo lo que es de César* (Promus, 1981).

the stubborn determination to keep pressing on toward a new and brighter dawn.

CONTRIBUTORS

Ana Maldonado is with the Frente Francisco Miranda (Venezuela).

Anya Parampil is a journalist at *The Grayzone.*

Belén Fernández is the author of *Exile: Rejecting America and Finding the World* (2019).

Carlos Ron is the President of Instituto Simón Bolívar (Caracas, Venezuela).

Claudia De La Cruz is Co-Executive Director of The People's Forum (New York).

George Ciccariello-Maher is the author of *Building the Commune: Radical Democracy in Venezuela* (2016).

Greg Wilpert is deputy editor at the Institute for New Economic Thinking and co-founder of Venezuelanalysis.com.

Joe Sammut lived and worked in Venezuela in 2014-15 and is now a Ph.D. candidate at Queen Mary University of London.

Manolo De Los Santos is Co-Executive Director of The People's Forum and a Researcher at Tricontinental: Institute for Social Research.

MIGUEL STÉDILE is a member of Front—Instituto de Estudos Contemporâneos and in the national coordination of Brazil's Landless Workers Movement.

PAOLA ESTRADA is a member of the Brazilian chapter of ALBA Movements and is part of the Secretariat of the International Peoples Assembly.

PRABHAT PATNAIK is a Professor Emeritus at the Centre for Economic Studies and Planning at Jawaharlal Nehru University (New Delhi, India).

SAMUEL MONCADA is the Permanent Representative of Venezuela to the United Nations.

VIJAY PRASHAD is the Executive Director of Tricontinental: Institute for Social Research and Chief Editor at LeftWord Books (India).

ZOE PC is an editor at *Peoples Dispatch*.

CPSIA information can be obtained
at www.ICGtesting.com
Printed in the USA
BVHW081240261120
594281BV00003B/317